Becoming a U.S. Citizen:

Understanding the Naturalization Process

Second Edition

BECOMING A U.S. CITIZEN

UNDERSTANDING THE NATURALIZATION PROCESS

Second Edition

PUBLISHING

New York

This publication is designed to provide accurate and authoritative information in regard to the subject matter covered. It is sold with the understanding that the publisher is not engaged in rendering legal, accounting, or other professional service. If legal advice or other expert assistance is required, the services of a competent professional should be sought.

Table of Contents

Step 5: Take the English Communication Practice Test

Step 6: Take the Civics Practice Test

How to Use This Book

Congratulations! You have made the decision to become a United States citizen. You may be at the point where you have a copy of Form N-400, the Application for Naturalization, from the U.S. Citizenship and Immigration Services (USCIS), or maybe you do not know where to start.

The naturalization process takes time and effort. You need to get the application, fill it out, and send it to the correct office with all of the necessary documents. Then you need to wait for a response, study for the English and civics tests, be fingerprinted, and have your picture taken—and that's before you go for your interview!

The purpose of this book is to explain each step of the process as simply as possible, guiding you as you make your way from applicant to citizen. However, you may come across words that you are not familiar with. Do not skip them and hope you will figure them out later; some of those words could make the difference between understanding what you need to do and making a mistake. It is very important that you take the time to look those words up in a dictionary, and write down the definitions to study later.

In addition, do not be tempted to skip any of the practice exercises. They are designed to show you what to expect during the interview and to teach you how to pass the English and civics tests and the interview itself. The tests in Steps 5 and 6 will reinforce what you learned in previous steps.

From time to time the USCIS makes changes in parts of the naturalization process. If you have questions, it is a good idea to check the USCIS website (www.uscis.gov) or to call them at 1-800-375-5283. The USCIS publishes the helpful *A Guide to the Naturalization Process* that you can order or download from the website.

The decision to become a U.S. citizen is an important one. This book will guide you through the process, from application to oath ceremony to citizenship. Good luck!

Step 1: **Understanding Citizenship, Naturalization, and Eligibility**

Before you begin the naturalization process, you need to understand it. Why should you become a naturalized citizen? How does the naturalization process work? Who can and cannot become a naturalized citizen? This section helps you take the first step; it gives you the answers to these important questions and more.

WHAT IS CITIZENSHIP?

Citizenship refers to the legal status of being a citizen. It differs from being an alien or a national in that citizenship status gives a person more rights within the United States. In addition to those rights, citizenship also comes with responsibilities.

Rights of U.S. citizens include:

- The right to vote

- The right to have a U.S. passport

- The right to obtain a federal government job

- The right to have U.S. government protection and help when traveling to other countries

- The right to petition the U.S. government to allow close relatives to come to America to live

Responsibilities of citizenship include:

- Giving up allegiances to other countries

- Supporting and defending the Constitution and U.S. laws

- Swearing allegiance to the United States

- Serving in the armed forces of the United States when required

- Registering to vote

- Voting

- Serving on a jury

- Tolerating the differences of other citizens

HOW CAN YOU BECOME A U.S. CITIZEN?

There are two ways to become a citizen: by birth and through the naturalization process.

You are a U.S. citizen by birth if you were born in the United States or born to U.S. citizens (even if you were born outside the country). If one parent is a U.S. citizen and that parent lived at least five years in the United States before you were born and at least two of those years were after his or her 14th birthday, you are born a U.S. citizen. People born in Puerto Rico, Guam, and the U.S. Virgin Islands are also citizens by birth.

If you were not born an American citizen, you must go through the naturalization process to become one. If you are 18 or older, you must apply for naturalization using Form N-400, Application for Naturalization. This book explains every step of the naturalization process, from requesting Form N-400 and filling it out, to studying for the English and civics tests.

ARE YOU ELIGIBLE FOR CITIZENSHIP VIA NATURALIZATION?

The naturalization process is open to most people who want to become citizens. Some of these people are already permanent residents, some are married to U.S. citizens, and others are serving or have served in the U.S. military. To be eligible for naturalization, these different groups must meet certain requirements.

General Requirements

No matter whether an applicant is in the military, works for an American company, is a permanent resident, or any other circumstance, everyone applying for naturalization must meet general requirements (although the details of those requirements may vary). Applicants must be at least 18 years old, and most must be permanent residents who have lived in the United States for a period of time, known as "continuous residence" and "physical presence" (see box below). In addition, most applicants must live in one district or state for a period of time (typically three months).

WHAT'S THE DIFFERENCE BETWEEN CONTINUOUS RESIDENCE AND PHYSICAL PRESENCE?

The continuous residence requirement refers to the number of days as a permanent resident that has not been broken by a trip of more than six months outside the United States. The physical presence requirement refers to the total number of days spent in the United States as a permanent resident.

It is possible to meet the continuous residence requirement but not the physical presence requirement. This could happen if an applicant takes so many shorter trips (less than six months each) that he or she is not in the United States for the number of days needed.

Every applicant must possess good moral character, which means he or she does not have a serious criminal record. There are no exceptions to this requirement. Applicants must also be willing to pledge an oath of allegiance to the United States and its Constitution. Other requirements include knowledge of U.S. history and its system of government (known together as "civics"); and the ability to write, read, and speak basic English.

WHAT IS A PERMANENT RESIDENT?

Once you enter the United States, you are not legally allowed to live and work in the country until you apply for and receive an immigrant visa (also called a "green card"). Immigrants with visas are known as permanent residents. Most people who apply for visas must have either a family member (who is already a U.S. citizen or permanent resident) or an employer sponsor them. For those without a sponsor, there is a green card "lottery." For more information about permanent resident status, check the website of the United States Citizenship and Immigration Services, www.uscis.gov.

For Permanent Residents

Most people applying for naturalization are permanent residents who have been so for at least five years and have no special circumstances. For these applicants, the requirements are:

- Continuous residence—At least five years with no trips outside the United States lasting six months or longer

- Physical presence—30 months

- Time in district or state—Three months

- English and civics tests—Required

- Oath of allegiance—Required

If you have been married to and living with an American citizen for at least three years, and your spouse has been an American citizen for those three years, you must meet these requirements:

- Continuous residence—At least three years with no trips outside the United States lasting six months or longer

- Physical presence—18 months

- Time in district or state—Three months

- English and civics tests—Required

- Oath of allegiance—Required

For Members, Employees, and Family Members of the Military

If you are in the U.S. Armed Forces (or were honorably discharged no longer than six months before filing your application) and have served for at least one year, you must be a permanent resident on the day of your interview. However, you do not need to meet requirements for continuous residence, physical presence, or time in district or state.

If you were honorably discharged more than six months ago, or served less than a year, your requirements are:

- Continuous residence—Five years as a permanent resident with no trips longer than six months (service overseas does not break the period of continuous residence)

- Physical presence—30 months (time spent in service overseas is included)

- Time in district or state—Three months

- English and civics tests—Required
- Oath of allegiance—Required

If you performed active duty military service during a war (see box below), you do not have to be a permanent resident (unless you did not enlist or re-enlist in the United States or its outlying possessions). There are also no requirements for continuous residence, physical presence, or time in district or state. However, you must pass the English and civics tests and take the oath of allegiance.

- World War I (November 11, 1916–April 6, 1917) ————
- World War II (September 1, 1939–December 31, 1946)
- Korea (June 25, 1950–July 1, 1955)
- Vietnam (February 28, 1961–October 15, 1978)
- Persian Gulf (August 2, 1990–April 11, 1991)
- On or after September 11, 2001

If you were married to a U.S. citizen who died during a period of honorable active duty service in the U.S. Armed Forces, and were married to and living with your spouse when he or she died, you must be a permanent resident on the day of your interview. There are no requirements for continuous residence, physical presence, or time in district or state, but you must pass the English and civics tests and take the oath of allegiance.

If you served on a vessel operated by the United States or on a vessel registered in the United States and owned by U.S. citizens or a U.S. corporation, you must meet the following requirements:

- Continuous residence—Five years as a permanent resident with no trips outside the United States longer than six months (time spent in service is treated as time spent inside the United States)

- Physical presence—30 months (time spent in service is treated as time spent inside the United States)

- Time in district or state—Three months

- English and civics tests—Required

- Oath of allegiance—Required

If you are an employee or an individual under contract to the U.S. government, your requirements are:

- Continuous residence—Five years as a permanent resident without leaving the United States for six months or longer (an absence for one year or more breaks continuous residence; maintaining continuous residence requires at least one year of unbroken continuous residence since becoming a permanent resident and an approved Application to Preserve Residence for Naturalization Purposes [Form N-470] before leaving the United States for a year)

- Physical presence—30 months (time spent outside the United States during this type of employment is considered time inside the United States as long as an N-470 is approved before leaving the United States for a year)

- Time in district or state—Three months

- English and civics tests—Required

- Oath of allegiance—Required

Other Special Considerations

There are several other exceptions to the general rules for naturalization, including special requirements for U.S. nationals, members of the clergy, employees of American companies, and spouses of American citizens in certain professions. Your age and/or disability may also play a role in determining what requirements you must meet to become a citizen.

U.S. Nationals

If you are a U.S. national (a noncitizen who owes permanent allegiance to the United States), are a resident of any state, and are otherwise qualified for naturalization, you do not need to have permanent resident status. However, you must fulfill continuous residence, physical presence, and time in district or state requirements. You must also pass the English and civics tests and take the oath of allegiance.

Clergy Members

If you perform ministerial or priestly functions for a religious denomination or an interdenominational organization with a valid presence in the United States, you must fulfill the following requirements:

- Continuous residence—Five years as a permanent resident without leaving the United States for trips of six months or longer (an absence for one year or more breaks continuous residence; maintaining continuous residence requires at least one year of unbroken continuous residence since becoming a permanent resident and an approved N-470 before leaving the United States for a year)

- Physical presence—30 months (time spent in this type of employment is considered time physically present in the United States if you get an approved N-470 before applying for naturalization)

- Time in district or state—Three months

- English and civics tests—Required

- Oath of allegiance—Required

Employees of U.S. Companies or Institutions

If you are an employee of an American institution of research recognized by the attorney general, an American-owned firm or corporation engaged in the development of foreign trade and commerce for the United States, or a public international organization of which the United States is a member by law or treaty (if the employment began after you became a permanent resident), you must meet these requirements:

- Continuous residence—Five years as a permanent resident without leaving the United States for six months or longer (an absence for one year or more breaks continuous residence; maintaining continuous residence requires at least one year of unbroken continuous residence since becoming a permanent resident and an approved N-470 before leaving the United States for a year)

- Physical presence—30 months

- Time in district or state—Three months

- English and civics tests—Required

- Oath of allegiance—Required

If you are an employee of a U.S. nonprofit organization that principally promotes the interests of the United States abroad through the communications media, and have been for at least five years, there are no requirements for continuous residence, physical presence, or time in district or state. However, you must pass the English and civics tests and take the oath of allegiance.

Spouses of U.S. Citizens with Special Considerations

You must be a permanent resident, pass the English and civics tests, and take the oath of allegiance, but you do not have to meet requirements for continuous residence, physical presence, or time in district or state if your spouse is a U.S. citizen working abroad under an employment contract with a qualifying employer from the following list for at least a year and will continue to work for that employer at the time you are naturalized. To qualify, your spouse must be

- a member of the U.S. Armed Forces;

- an employee or individual under contract to the U.S. government;

- an employee of an American research institution recognized by the attorney general;

- an employee of an American-owned firm or corporation that works to develop foreign trade and commerce for the United States;

- an employee of a public international organization of which the United States is a member by law or treaty; or

- a person who performs ministerial or priestly functions for a religious denomination or an interdenominational organization with a valid presence in the United States.

Exceptions for Age and Disabilities

If you are over the age of 50 and have lived in the United States as a permanent resident for 20 years or more, or are over the age of 55 and have lived in the United States as a permanent resident for at least 15 years, you must meet requirements for continuous residence, physical presence, and time in district or state. However, you can take the civics test in the language of your choice, and you do not have to take the English test.

If you are over 65 and have lived in the United States as a permanent resident for at least 20 years, you must meet requirements for continuous residence, physical presence, and time in district or state. You may take an easier version of the civics test in the language of your choice, and do not have to take the English test.

If you have a physical, developmental, or mental disability or impairment, you can apply for an exception to the English and civics requirements by filing Form N-648, Medical Certification for Disability Exceptions, with your application.

I'M CONFUSED. WHO CAN ANSWER MY QUESTIONS? ————

If you need help as you go through the naturalization process, check the following:

- USCIS website—The USCIS website (www.uscis.gov) explains how to become a citizen and offers *A Guide to the Naturalization Process* and Form N-400 to download.

- Local USCIS office—There is an information counter at every USCIS office where an employee is available to answer your questions.

- USCIS National Customer Service Center—Call 1-800-375-5283 if you live in the continental United States for basic information about the naturalization process. You can order forms, find out the status of an application, and get advice before you file an application.

- Community-based organizations (CBOs)—There are many groups across the country that work to help people who want to become citizens. They help immigrants learn English and U.S. history and offer help filling out Form N-400. Some CBOs reach out to immigrants of specific races or ethnic backgrounds (such as those listed in the Congressional Hispanic Caucus Institute's Regional and Local Hispanic Organization Directory at www.chci.org/publications/pdf/directory/regional_orgs-1.pdf), and others are smaller and more local and help whoever is in need. To find a CBO, check the phonebook under "Immigration and Naturalization" or search the Internet. Other immigrants can also be a good source of information.

- Immigration lawyers—Lawyers who specialize in immigration law can answer your questions about eligibility and other issues. You may be able to find an immigration lawyer in your local phonebook; check under "Lawyer" or "Attorney," and under "Immigration and Naturalization." The American Immigration Law Foundation has an immigration lawyer referral service that can also help. Send an email to ilrs@aila.org or call 1-800-954-0254. They will give you the name of an attorney in your area who can help, and who will charge no more than $100 for a half-hour consultation.

NOTES

_____

_____

_____

_____

_____

_____

_____

_____

_____

_____

_____

_____

_____

_____

_____

_____

_____

_____

_____

_____

_____

_____

_____

_____

_____

_____

_____

_____

_____

_____

_____

_____

_____

_____

_____

_____

_____

_____

_____

_____

_____

_____

_____

_____

_____

_____

_____

_____

_____

_____

_____

_____

_____

_____

_____

_____

_____

_____

_____

_____

_____

_____

_____

_____

_____

_____

_____

_____

_____

_____

_____

_____

_____

_____

_____

_____

_____

_____

_____

_____

_____

_____

_____

_____

_____

_____

_____

_____

Step 2: **Applying for Naturalized Citizenship**

In this step, you learn everything you need to know to apply for citizenship, including how to fill out your application and how to prepare for your interview. Follow the directions carefully, and be sure to read over your application. If you make a mistake, the time it takes to process your application will be much longer than it needs to be.

When you have determined that you are eligible for citizenship, you need to get a copy of the application, called Form N-400. There are two ways to get N-400: You can call the USCIS and have them send a copy to you, or you can download the form from the Internet. The toll-free phone number for the USCIS is 1-800-375-5283, and their Internet address is www.uscis.gov.

FILLING OUT THE FORM

When you fill out Form N-400 (Figure 2.1), complete each section. Do not leave anything blank, or the processing of your application will take longer. Answer everything honestly. All of the information on your application can be questioned during your interview. If the USCIS finds out that you did not tell the truth on your application or during your interview, your application will be denied.

PHOTOGRAPHS AND REQUIRED DOCUMENTS

After you complete your application, you need to get four color passport-style photographs taken of yourself (two will be sent with your application and two should be brought to your interview). The photos must be full-frontal, meaning you are looking straight at the camera. Your facial features must be showing, even if your religion requires you to wear a head covering. Do not wear glasses or earrings. The photos must be identical, and must have your "A" number written on the back lightly in pencil. To see an example of an acceptable photo, check http://www.uscis.gov/files/nativedocuments/M-603.pdf or call the USCIS toll-free at 1-800-375-5283 to request a copy of the photo flyer.

In addition to two photographs, you must also send a copy of both sides of your permanent resident card (also called the alien registration receipt card or green card). If you have lost your card, send a copy of the receipt of your Form I-90, Application to Replace Alien Registration Receipt Card. Finally, include a check or money order for the application fee and the fingerprinting fee with your "A" number written on the back.

If there is any part of the oath of allegiance (see page 41) that you cannot say because of religious beliefs or because a physical or mental disability prevents you from understanding it, you must include a letter with your application that explains your situation. For more information on modified oaths, see the section "The Loyalty Oath Ceremony" on page 41. Copies of other documents may be required for special circumstances. Read the following list carefully to determine whether any of the circumstances apply to you.

- If an attorney or accredited representative is acting on your behalf, send a completed original Form G-28, Notice of Entry of Appearance as Attorney or Representative.

- If your current legal name is different from the name on your permanent resident card, send the document(s) that legally changed your name (marriage certificate, divorce decree, or other court document).

Figure 2.1 Form N-400

OMB No. 1615-0052; Expires 12/31/09

Department of Homeland Security
U.S Citizenship and Immigration Services

N-400 Application
for Naturalization

Clearly or type your answers using CAPITAL letters. Failure to print clearly may delay your application. Use black ink.

Part 1. Your Name *(Person applying for naturalization)*

Write your USCIS A'- number here:
A

A. Your current legal name.

Family Name *(Last Name)*

Given Name *(First Name)*   Full Middle Name *(If applicable)*

For USCIS Use Only

Bar Code	Date Stamp

B. Your name exactly as it appears on your Permanent Resident Card.

Family Name *(Last Name)*

Given Name *(First Name)*   Full Middle Name *(If applicable)*

Remarks

C. If you have ever used other names, provide them below.

Family Name *(Last Name)*	Given Name *(First Name)*	Middle Name

D. Name change *(optional)*

Read the Instructions before you decide whether to change your name.

1. Would you like to legally change your name? ☐ Yes ☐ No

2. If "Yes," print the new name you would like to use. Do not use initials or abbreviations when writing your new name.

Family Name *(Last Name)*

Given Name *(First Name)*   Full Middle Name

Action Block

Part 2. Information About Your Eligibility *(Check only one)*

I am at least 18 years old AND

A. ☐ I have been a lawful permanent resident of the United States for at least five years.

B. ☐ I have been a lawful permanent resident of the United States for at least three years, and I have been married to and living with the same U.S. citizen for the last three years, and my spouse has been a U.S. citizen for the last three years.

C. ☐ I am applying on the basis of qualifying military service.

D. ☐ Other *(Explain)* _____

Form N-400 (Rev. 01/22/09) Y

Source: www.uscis.gov

Figure 2.1   Form N-400 (continued)

Part 3. Information About You	Write your USCIS A- number here: A

A. U.S. Social Security Number   **B.** Date of Birth *(mm/dd/yyyy)*   **C.** Date You Became a Permanent Resident *(mm/dd/yyyy)*

D. Country of Birth   **E.** Country of Nationality

F. Are either of your parents U.S. citizens? *(If yes, see instructions)*   ☐ Yes   ☐ No

G. What is your current marital status?   ☐ Single, Never Married   ☐ Married   ☐ Divorced   ☐ Widowed

☐ Marriage Annulled or Other *(Explain)*

H. Are you requesting a waiver of the English and/or U.S. History and Government requirements based on a disability or impairment and attaching Form N-648 with your application?   ☐ Yes   ☐ No

I. Are you requesting an accommodation to the naturalization process because of a disability or impairment? *(See instructions for some examples of accommodations.)*   ☐ Yes   ☐ No

If you answered "Yes," check the box below that applies:

☐ I am deaf or hearing impaired and need a sign language interpreter who uses the following language: _____

☐ I use a wheelchair.

☐ I am blind or sight impaired.

☐ I will need another type of accommodation. Explain: _____

Part 4. Addresses and Telephone Numbers

A. Home Address - Street Number and Name *(Do not write a P.O. Box in this space.)*   Apartment Number

City   County   State   ZIP Code   Country

B. Care of   Mailing Address - Street Number and Name *(If different from home address)*   Apartment Number

City   State   ZIP Code   Country

C. Daytime Phone Number *(If any)*   Evening Phone Number *(If any)*   E-Mail Address *(If any)*

(   )   (   )

Form N-400 (Rev. 01/22/09) Y Page 2

Figure 2.1   Form N-400 (continued)

Part 5. Information for Criminal Records Search	Write your USCIS A-number here: A

NOTE: The categories below are those required by the FBI. See instructions for more information.

A. Gender

☐ Male   ☐ Female

B. Height

Feet	Inches

C. Weight

Pounds

D. Are you Hispanic or Latino?   ☐ Yes   ☐ No

E. Race *(Select one or more)*

☐ White   ☐ Asian   ☐ Black or African American   ☐ American Indian or Alaskan Native   ☐ Native Hawaiian or Other Pacific Islander

F. Hair color

☐ Black   ☐ Brown   ☐ Blonde   ☐ Gray   ☐ White   ☐ Red   ☐ Sandy   ☐ Bald (No Hair)

G. Eye color

☐ Brown   ☐ Blue   ☐ Green   ☐ Hazel   ☐ Gray   ☐ Black   ☐ Pink   ☐ Maroon   ☐ Other

Part 6. Information About Your Residence and Employment

A. Where have you lived during the last five years? Begin with where you live now and then list every place you lived for the last five years. If you need more space, use a separate sheet of paper.

Street Number and Name, Apartment Number, City, State, Zip Code, and Country	Dates *(mm/dd/yyyy)*	
	From	To
Current Home Address - Same as Part 4.A		Present

B. Where have you worked (or, if you were a student, what schools did you attend) during the last five years? Include military service. Begin with your current or latest employer and then list every place you have worked or studied for the last five years. If you need more space, use a separate sheet of paper.

Employer or School Name	Employer or School Address *(Street, City, and State)*	Dates *(mm/dd/yyyy)*		Your Occupation
		From	To	

Form N-400 (Rev. 01/22/09) Y Page 3

KAPLAN

Figure 2.1   Form N-400 (continued)

Part 7. Time Outside the United States	Write your USCIS A- number here:
(Including Trips to Canada, Mexico and the Caribbean Islands)	A

A. How many total days did you spend outside of the United States during the past five years? ____ days

B. How many trips of 24 hours or more have you taken outside of the United States during the past five years? ____ trips

C. List below all the trips of 24 hours or more that you have taken outside of the United States since becoming a lawful permanent resident. Begin with your most recent trip. If you need more space, use a separate sheet of paper.

Date You Left the United States *(mm/dd/yyyy)*	Date You Returned to the United States *(mm/dd/yyyy)*	Did Trip Last Six Months or More?	Countries to Which You Traveled	Total Days Out of the United States
		☐ Yes ☐ No		
		☐ Yes ☐ No		
		☐ Yes ☐ No		
		☐ Yes ☐ No		
		☐ Yes ☐ No		
		☐ Yes ☐ No		
		☐ Yes ☐ No		
		☐ Yes ☐ No		
		☐ Yes ☐ No		
		☐ Yes ☐ No		

Part 8. Information About Your Marital History

A. How many times have you been married (including annulled marriages)? ____ If you have never been married, go to Part 9.

B. If you are now married, give the following information about your spouse:

1. Spouse's Family Name *(Last Name)*   Given Name *(First Name)*   Full Middle Name *(If applicable)*

2. Date of Birth *(mm/dd/yyyy)*   3. Date of Marriage *(mm/dd/yyyy)*   4. Spouse's U.S. Social Security #

5. Home Address - Street Number and Name   Apartment Number

City   State   Zip Code

Form N-400 (Rev. 01/22/09) Y Page 4

Figure 2.1   Form N-400 (continued)

Part 8. Information About Your Marital History *(Continued)*	Write your USCIS A- number here: A

C. Is your spouse a U.S. citizen?   ☐ Yes   ☐ No

D. If your spouse is a U.S. citizen, give the following information:

    1. When did your spouse become a U.S. citizen?   ☐ At Birth   ☐ Other

    If "Other," give the following information:

    2. Date your spouse became a U.S. citizen

    3. Place your spouse became a U.S. citizen *(See instructions)*

          City and State

E. If your spouse is not a U.S. citizen, give the following information :

    1. Spouse's Country of Citizenship

    2. Spouse's USCIS A- Number *(If applicable)*   A

    3. Spouse's Immigration Status

    ☐ Lawful Permanent Resident   ☐ Other

F. If you were married before, provide the following information about your prior spouse. If you have more than one previous marriage, use a separate sheet of paper to provide the information requested in Questions 1-5 below.

    1. Prior Spouse's Family Name *(Last Name)*   Given Name *(First Name)*   Full Middle Name *(If applicable)*

    2. Prior Spouse's Immigration Status

    ☐ U.S. Citizen
    ☐ Lawful Permanent Resident
    ☐ Other

    3. Date of Marriage *(mm/dd/yyyy)*   4. Date Marriage Ended *(mm/dd/yyyy)*

    5. How Marriage Ended

    ☐ Divorce   ☐ Spouse Died   ☐ Other

G. How many times has your current spouse been married (including annulled marriages)? ☐

    If your spouse has ever been married before, give the following information about your spouse's prior marriage.
    If your spouse has more than one previous marriage, use a separate sheet(s) of paper to provide the information requested in Questions 1 - 5 below.

    1. Prior Spouse's Family Name *(Last Name)*   Given Name *(First Name)*   Full Middle Name *(If applicable)*

    2. Prior Spouse's Immigration Status

    ☐ U.S. Citizen
    ☐ Lawful Permanent Resident
    ☐ Other

    3. Date of Marriage *(mm/dd/yyyy)*   4. Date Marriage Ended *(mm/dd/yyyy)*

    5. How Marriage Ended

    ☐ Divorce   ☐ Spouse Died   ☐ Other

Form N-400 (Rev. 01/22/09) Y Page 5

Figure 2.1   Form N-400 (continued)

Part 9. Information About Your Children	Write your USCIS A- number here: A

A. How many sons and daughters have you had? For more information on which sons and daughters you should include and how to complete this section, see the Instructions.

B. Provide the following information about all of your sons and daughters. If you need more space, use a separate sheet of paper.

Full Name of Son or Daughter	Date of Birth (mm/dd/yyyy)	USCIS A- number (if child has one)	Country of Birth	Current Address (Street, City, State and Country)
		A		
		A		
		A		
		A		
		A		
		A		
		A		
		A		

Add Children		Go to continuation page

Part 10. Additional Questions

Answer Questions 1 through 14. If you answer "Yes" to any of these questions, include a written explanation with this form. Your written explanation should (1) explain why your answer was "Yes" and (2) provide any additional information that helps to explain your answer.

A. General Questions.

1. Have you ever claimed to be a U.S. citizen *(in writing or any other way)*?   ☐ Yes   ☐ No

2. Have you ever registered to vote in any Federal, State, or local election in the United States?   ☐ Yes   ☐ No

3. Have you ever voted in any Federal, State, or local election in the United States?   ☐ Yes   ☐ No

4. Since becoming a lawful permanent resident, have you ever failed to file a required Federal, State, or local tax return?   ☐ Yes   ☐ No

5. Do you owe any Federal, State, or local taxes that are overdue?   ☐ Yes   ☐ No

6. Do you have any title of nobility in any foreign country?   ☐ Yes   ☐ No

7. Have you ever been declared legally incompetent or been confined to a mental institution within the last five years?   ☐ Yes   ☐ No

Form N-400 (Rev. 01/22/09) Y Page 6

Figure 2.1   Form N-400 (continued)

Form N-400 (Rev. 01/22/09) Y Page 7

Part 10. Additional Questions *(Continued)*	Write your USCIS A- number here: A

B. Affiliations.

8. a Have you ever been a member of or associated with any organization, association, fund foundation, party, club, society, or similar group in the United States or in any other place?   ☐ Yes ☐ No

b. If you answered "Yes," list the name of each group below. If you need more space, attach the names of the other group(s) on a separate sheet of paper.

Name of Group	Name of Group
1.	6.
2.	7.
3.	8.
4.	9.
5.	10.

9. Have you ever been a member of or in any way associated *(either directly or indirectly)* with:

a. The Communist Party?   ☐ Yes ☐ No

b. Any other totalitarian party?   ☐ Yes ☐ No

c. A terrorist organization?   ☐ Yes ☐ No

10. Have you ever advocated *(either directly or indirectly)* the overthrow of any government by force or violence?   ☐ Yes ☐ No

11. Have you ever persecuted *(either directly or indirectly)* any person because of race, religion, national origin, membership in a particular social group, or political opinion?   ☐ Yes ☐ No

12. Between March 23, 1933, and May 8, 1945, did you work for or associate in any way *(either directly or indirectly)* with:

a. The Nazi government of Germany?   ☐ Yes ☐ No

b. Any government in any area (1) occupied by, (2) allied with, or (3) established with the help of the Nazi government of Germany?   ☐ Yes ☐ No

c. Any German, Nazi, or S.S. military unit, paramilitary unit, self-defense unit, vigilante unit, citizen unit, police unit, government agency or office, extermination camp, concentration camp, prisoner of war camp, prison, labor camp, or transit camp?   ☐ Yes ☐ No

C. Continuous Residence.

Since becoming a lawful permanent resident of the United States:

13. Have you ever called yourself a "nonresident" on a Federal, State, or local tax return?   ☐ Yes ☐ No

14. Have you ever failed to file a Federal, State, or local tax return because you considered yourself to be a "nonresident"?   ☐ Yes ☐ No

Figure 2.1 Form N-400 (continued)

Part 10. Additional Questions *(continued)*	Write your USCIS A- number here: A

D. Good Moral Character.

For the purposes of this application, you must answer "Yes" to the following questions, if applicable, even if your records were sealed or otherwise cleared or if anyone, including a judge, law enforcement officer, or attorney, told you that you no longer have a record.

15. Have you ever committed a crime or offense for which you were not arrested? ☐ Yes ☐ No

16. Have you ever been arrested, cited, or detained by any law enforcement officer (including USCIS or former INS and military officers) for any reason? ☐ Yes ☐ No

17. Have you ever been charged with committing any crime or offense? ☐ Yes ☐ No

18. Have you ever been convicted of a crime or offense? ☐ Yes ☐ No

19. Have you ever been placed in an alternative sentencing or a rehabilitative program (for example: diversion, deferred prosecution, withheld adjudication, deferred adjudication)? ☐ Yes ☐ No

20. Have you ever received a suspended sentence, been placed on probation, or been paroled? ☐ Yes ☐ No

21. Have you ever been in jail or prison? ☐ Yes ☐ No

If you answered "Yes" to any of Questions 15 through 21, complete the following table. If you need more space, use a separate sheet of paper to give the same information.

Why were you arrested, cited, detained, or charged?	Date arrested, cited, detained, or charged? *(mm/dd/yyyy)*	Where were you arrested, cited, detained, or charged? *(City, State, Country)*	Outcome or disposition of the arrest, citation, detention, or charge *(No charges filed, charges dismissed, jail, probation, etc.)*

Answer Questions 22 through 33. If you answer "Yes" to any of these questions, attach (1) your written explanation why your answer was "Yes" and (2) any additional information or documentation that helps explain your answer.

22. Have you ever:

    a. Been a habitual drunkard? ☐ Yes ☐ No

    b. Been a prostitute, or procured anyone for prostitution? ☐ Yes ☐ No

    c. Sold or smuggled controlled substances, illegal drugs, or narcotics? ☐ Yes ☐ No

    d. Been married to more than one person at the same time? ☐ Yes ☐ No

    e. Helped anyone enter or try to enter the United States illegally? ☐ Yes ☐ No

    f. Gambled illegally or received income from illegal gambling? ☐ Yes ☐ No

    g. Failed to support your dependents or to pay alimony? ☐ Yes ☐ No

23. Have you ever given false or misleading information to any U.S. Government official while applying for any immigration benefit or to prevent deportation, exclusion, or removal? ☐ Yes ☐ No

24. Have you ever lied to any U.S. Government official to gain entry or admission into the United States? ☐ Yes ☐ No

---

Figure 2.1   Form N-400 (continued)

Part 10. Additional Questions *(Continued)*	Write your USCIS A- number here: A

E.   Removal, Exclusion, and Deportation Proceedings.

25. Are removal, exclusion, rescission, or deportation proceedings pending against you?   ☐ Yes   ☐ No

26. Have you ever been removed, excluded, or deported from the United States?   ☐ Yes   ☐ No

27. Have you ever been ordered to be removed, excluded, or deported from the United States?   ☐ Yes   ☐ No

28. Have you ever applied for any kind of relief from removal, exclusion, or deportation?   ☐ Yes   ☐ No

F. Military Service.

29. Have you ever served in the U.S. Armed Forces?   ☐ Yes   ☐ No

30. Have you ever left the United States to avoid being drafted into the U.S. Armed Forces?   ☐ Yes   ☐ No

31. Have you ever applied for any kind of exemption from military service in the U.S. Armed Forces?   ☐ Yes   ☐ No

32. Have you ever deserted from the U.S. Armed Forces?   ☐ Yes   ☐ No

G. Selective Service Registration.

33. Are you a male who lived in the United States at any time between your 18th and 26th birthdays   ☐ Yes   ☐ No
in any status except as a lawful nonimmigrant?
If you answered "NO," go on to question 34.

If you answered "YES," provide the information below.

If you answered "YES," but you did not register with the Selective Service System and are still under 26 years of age, you must register before you apply for naturalization, so that you can complete the information below:

Date Registered (mm/dd/yyyy) [   ]   Selective Service Number [   ]

If you answered "YES," but you did not register with the Selective Service and you are now 26 years old or older, attach a statement explaining why you did not register.

H. Oath Requirements. *(See Part 14 for the text of the oath)*

Answer Questions 34 through 39. If you answer "No" to any of these questions, attach (1) your written explanation why the answer was "No" and (2) any additional information or documentation that helps to explain your answer.

34. Do you support the Constitution and form of government of the United States?   ☐ Yes   ☐ No

35. Do you understand the full Oath of Allegiance to the United States?   ☐ Yes   ☐ No

36. Are you willing to take the full Oath of Allegiance to the United States?   ☐ Yes   ☐ No

37. If the law requires it, are you willing to bear arms on behalf of the United States?   ☐ Yes   ☐ No

38. If the law requires it, are you willing to perform noncombatant services in the U.S. Armed Forces?   ☐ Yes   ☐ No

39. If the law requires it, are you willing to perform work of national importance under civilian direction?   ☐ Yes   ☐ No

Form N-400 (Rev. 01/22/09) Y Page 9

Figure 2.1   Form N-400 (continued)

Part 11. Your Signature

Write your USCIS A- number here:
A

I certify, under penalty of perjury under the laws of the United States of America, that this application, and the evidence submitted with it, are all true and correct. I authorize the release of any information that the USCIS needs to determine my eligibility for naturalization.

Your Signature

Date *(mm/dd/yyyy)*

Part 12. Signature of Person Who Prepared This Application for You *(If applicable)*

I declare under penalty of perjury that I prepared this application at the request of the above person. The answers provided are based on information of which I have personal knowledge and/or were provided to me by the above named person in response to the *exact questions* contained on this form.

Preparer's Printed Name

Preparer's Signature

Date *(mm/dd/yyyy)*

Preparer's Firm or Organization Name *(If applicable)*

Preparer's Daytime Phone Number

Preparer's Address - Street Number and Name

City

State

Zip Code

NOTE: Do not complete Parts 13 and 14 until a USCIS Officer instructs you to do so.

Part 13. Signature at Interview

I swear (affirm) and certify under penalty of perjury under the laws of the United States of America that I know that the contents of this application for naturalization subscribed by me, including corrections numbered 1 through _____ and the evidence submitted by me numbered pages 1 through _____ , are true and correct to the best of my knowledge and belief.

Subscribed to and sworn to (affirmed) before me

Officer's Printed Name or Stamp

Date *(mm/dd/yyyy)*

Complete Signature of Applicant

Officer's Signature

Part 14. Oath of Allegiance

If your application is approved, you will be scheduled for a public oath ceremony at which time you will be required to take the following Oath of Allegiance immediately prior to becoming a naturalized citizen. By signing, you acknowledge your willingness and ability to take this oath:

I hereby declare, on oath, that I absolutely and entirely renounce and abjure all allegiance and fidelity to any foreign prince, potentate, state, or sovereignty, of whom or which I have heretofore been a subject or citizen;

that I will support and defend the Constitution and laws of the United States of America against all enemies, foreign and domestic;

that I will bear true faith and allegiance to the same;

that I will bear arms on behalf of the United States when required by the law;

that I will perform noncombatant service in the Armed Forces of the United States when required by the law;

that I will perform work of national importance under civilian direction when required by the law; and

that I take this obligation freely, without any mental reservation or purpose of evasion, so help me God.

Printed Name of Applicant

Complete Signature of Applicant

Form N-400 (Rev. 01/22/09) Y Page 10

If you are applying for naturalization on the basis of marriage to a U.S. citizen, send the following four things:

1. Evidence that your spouse has been a U.S. citizen for the last three years:

   • birth certificate (if your spouse never lost citizenship since birth);

   • naturalization certificate;

   • certificate of citizenship;

   • the inside of the front cover and signature page of your spouse's current U.S. passport; or

   • form FS240, Report of Birth Abroad of a Citizen of the United States of America.

2. Your current marriage certificate

3. Proof of termination of all prior marriages of your spouse [divorce decree(s), annulment(s), or death certificate(s)]

4. Documents referring to you and your spouse:

   • tax returns, bank accounts, leases, mortgages, or birth certificates of children; or

   • Internal Revenue Service-certified copies of the income tax forms that you both filed for the past three years; or

   • an IRS tax return transcript for the last three years:

      • If you were married before, send proof that all earlier marriages ended [divorce decree(s), annulment(s), or death certificate(s)].

      • If you were previously in the U.S. military, send a completed original Form G-325B, Biographic Information.

- If you are currently in U.S. military service and are seeking citizenship based on that service, send a completed original Form N-426, Request for Certification of Military or Naval Service; and a completed original Form G-325B, Biographic Information.

- If you have taken any trip outside of the United States that lasted for six months or more since becoming a permanent resident, send evidence that you (and your family) continued to live, work, and/or keep ties to the United States, such as:

  - an IRS tax return "transcript" or an IRS-certified tax return listing tax information for the last five years (or for the last three years if you are applying on the basis of marriage to a U.S. citizen); or

  - rent or mortgage payments and pay stubs.

- If you have a dependent spouse or children who do not live with you, send

  1. any court or government order to provide financial support; and

  2. evidence of your financial support (including evidence that you have complied with any court or government order), such as:

     - cancelled checks;

     - money order receipts;

     - a court or agency printout of child support payments;

     - evidence of wage garnishments; or

     - a letter from the parent or guardian who cares for your children.

- If you answer "Yes" to any of questions 1 through 15 in Part 7, send a written explanation on a separate sheet of paper.

- If you answer "No" to any of questions 1 through 5 in Part 8, send a written explanation on a separate sheet of paper.

- If you have ever been arrested or detained by any law enforcement officer for any reason, and no charges were filed, send an original official statement by the arresting agency or applicable court confirming that no charges were filed.

- If you have ever been arrested or detained by any law enforcement officer for any reason, and charges were filed, send an original or court-certified copy of the complete arrest record and disposition for each incident (dismissal order, conviction record, or acquittal order).

- If you have ever been convicted or placed in an alternative sentencing program or rehabilitative program (such as a drug treatment or community service program), send an original or court-certified copy of the sentencing record for each incident, and evidence that you completed your sentence (an original or certified copy of your probation or parole record, or evidence that you completed an alternative sentencing program or rehabilitative program).

- If you have ever had any arrest or conviction vacated, set aside, sealed, expunged, or otherwise removed from your record, send an original or court-certified copy of the court order vacating, setting aside, sealing, expunging, or otherwise removing the arrest or conviction, or an original statement from the court that no record exists of your arrest or conviction.

- If you have ever failed to file an income tax return since you became a permanent resident, send all correspondence with the IRS regarding your failure to file.

- If you have any federal, state, or local taxes that are overdue, send a signed agreement from the IRS or state or local tax office showing that you have filed a tax return and arranged to pay the taxes you owe; and documentation from the IRS or state or local tax office showing the current status of your repayment program.

- If you are applying for a disability exception to the testing requirement, send an original Form N-648, Medical Certification for Disability Exceptions, completed less than six months ago by a licensed medical or osteopathic doctor or licensed clinical psychologist.

- If you did not register with the Selective Service and you are male, are 26 years old or older, and lived in the United States in a status other than as a lawful nonimmigrant between the ages of 18 and 26, send a Status Information Letter from the Selective Service (call 1-847-688-6888 for more information).

PROCESSING FEES

Currently, the fees for processing your N-400 are $595.00 for filing and $80.00 to process your fingerprints—and also your photograph and signature (if necessary). The fingerprint, or biometrics, fee is not required if you are 75 years or older, and the filing fee is not required if you are filing through service in the U.S. Armed Forces. If you are filing from abroad, the USCIS will tell you where to have your fingerprints taken, and a fee will be collected at the time of the fingerprinting. The application fees are not refundable even if your case is denied or you withdraw your application.

Include a check or money order (not cash) for $675.00 ($595.00 if you are 75 or older or if filing from abroad) payable to the "U.S. Department of Homeland Security." Write your "A" number on the back of the check or money order.

If you are a resident of Guam, make the fee payable to the "Treasurer, Guam." If you are a resident of the U.S. Virgin Islands, make the fee payable to the "Commissioner of Finance of the Virgin Islands."

If you are not able to pay these fees, you will need to send a declaration that states that you are unable to pay which must include the sentence "I declare under penalty of perjury that the foregoing is true and correct," and be signed and dated by you. With the declaration you must send documents proving why you cannot afford the fees. These can include documents that prove you are receiving benefits such as food stamps or Medicare, proof of a disability, or an income tax return showing that your income is at or below the poverty level. Write on your envelope, declaration, and supporting documents in large letters the words "fee waiver request."

HOLD THAT ENVELOPE!

Before you seal your application in an envelope, make a copy of it. Why? During your interview with a USCIS officer, he or she asks you questions about your application, so it makes sense to review it before the interview—you can even bring it with you to the interview, but you can't use it to prepare if you mail your only copy.

WHERE TO SEND YOUR APPLICATION

When you have completed your application, and have your photographs, required documents, and fees ready, mail them to one of the following locations, depending on where you live.

If you live in:	Send your application to:
Alabama	USCIS
Arkansas	P.O. Box 299026
Connecticut	Lewisville, TX 75029
Delaware	
District of Columbia	
Florida	
Georgia	
Kentucky	
Louisiana	
Maine	
Maryland	
Massachusetts	
Mississippi	
New Hampshire	
New Jersey	
New Mexico	
New York	
North Carolina	
Oklahoma	
Pennsylvania	
Rhode Island	
South Carolina	
Tennessee	
Texas	
Vermont	
Virginia	
West Virginia	
Puerto Rico	
U.S. Virgin Islands	

If you live in:	Send your application to:
Alaska Arizona California Colorado Hawaii Idaho Illinois Indiana Iowa Kansas Michigan Minnesota Missouri Montana Nebraska Nevada North Dakota Ohio Oregon South Dakota Utah Washington Wisconsin Wyoming Guam Commonwealth of the Northern Mariana Islands	Nebraska Service Center P.O. Box 87400 Lincoln, Nebraska 68501-7400

If you are serving in the military and filing under the military provisions, section 328 or 329, send your application (no matter where you are living or serving) to:

Nebraska Service Center
P.O. Box 87426
Lincoln, NE 68501-7426

YOUR FINGERPRINTING APPOINTMENT

After you file your application, you will get a letter telling you when and where to have your fingerprints taken. Most fingerprints are taken at application support centers or police departments. If you do not live near a fingerprinting location, the USCIS may send a van to your area in which to take fingerprints. If you are filing from abroad, the USCIS directs you to a U.S. consular office to be fingerprinted.

On the day you are to have your fingerprints taken, bring the letter you received from the USCIS, your permanent resident card, and another form of identification with a picture on it (driver's license, passport, or state identification card).

When you arrive at the fingerprinting location, your documents are checked and your fingerprints taken, usually with ink. Some sites now use electronic technology to take the prints without ink, and eventually all sites will use this technology. Your fingerprints are then sent to the FBI for a criminal background check.

WHAT IT MEANS IF YOUR FINGERPRINTS ARE REJECTED

Sometimes the FBI rejects fingerprints because they are not clear enough to read. If this happens, the USCIS sends you a letter telling you when to go back to the fingerprinting site. You are not charged another fingerprinting fee. If the FBI rejects your fingerprints again, you may need to contact the police departments in every place you have lived during the past five years to get police clearances. These clearances tell the FBI that you did not commit any crimes.

WHAT TO EXPECT AT THE INTERVIEW

The USCIS notifies you by mail regarding when and where to go for your interview. It is therefore very important that the USCIS has your correct address; let them know any time your address changes. If you cannot get to the interview, write to the office where it is scheduled and ask for a new date. Because rescheduling can add many months to the naturalization process, it is best to go to the first scheduled interview. If you do reschedule, the USCIS mails you a new notice with the rescheduled date. If you do not reschedule, and do not go to the interview, your case is closed. You then have one year to write to the USCIS and ask that your case be reopened. If you wait longer than one year, you have to file a new application (and pay fees again) to restart the naturalization process.

On the day of your interview, bring your permanent resident card or alien registration card, your passport (even if expired), and re-entry permits if you have them. If you were asked in the interview letter to bring other documents, make sure you have them with you. If you do not bring all of the documents requested by the USCIS, your application could be delayed or denied.

BEING PLACED UNDER OATH

At the start of your interview, the USCIS officer asks you to swear or promise that everything you say is true. Once you make that promise, you are "under oath." If you tell the officer something that is not true when under oath, your application will be denied. Because the officer asks you questions about your application, it is very important to tell the truth on the application as well as in your interview. If the USCIS finds out that you have said or written something that is not true after you have become a citizen, they can take away your citizenship.

Get to the office early and let the person at the front desk know that you are there. When it is time for your interview, a USCIS officer checks your documents and asks you questions about your application. He or she wants to know where you are from, where you live, how long you have lived there, your moral character, and your willingness to take an oath of allegiance to the United States.

WHO CAN COME WITH YOU TO YOUR INTERVIEW?

If you do not have to meet the English requirements (you are over 50 years old and have lived in the United States as a permanent resident for at least 20 years; over 55 years old and have lived in the United States as a permanent resident for at least 15 years; or if you have a disability that qualifies as a medical exemption), you can bring an interpreter to your interview.

If you want to bring your attorney or another representative, you must send Form G-28, Notice of Entry of Appearance as Attorney or Representative, with your application.

If you have a disability, you can bring a family member or legal guardian.

If you do not have a disability and plan to take the English test, you may bring someone with you to the USCIS office, but that person is not allowed in the interview room. Because it is often crowded in USCIS offices, it is best to bring someone with you only if necessary.

THE ENGLISH AND CIVICS TESTS

Your interview tests your knowledge of English and civics (U.S. history and government). Steps 3 and 4 explain everything you need to know to pass the English and civics tests, including how the English and civics tests are given. Study the steps carefully, and complete all of the practice exercises. Steps 5 and 6 provide more opportunities for practice, including English read-aloud exercises and questions based on Form N-400.

Some people may not have to take one or both tests because of age or disability. If you are over 50 years old and have lived in the United States as a permanent resident for at least 20 years, or are over 55 years old and have lived as a permanent resident for at least 15 years, you do not have to take the English test, but do have to take a civics test in your own language. If you are over 65 years old and have been a permanent resident for at least 20 years, you receive a simpler civics test in your choice of language.

People with some kinds of disabilities may be exempt from the English and civics tests. To get this exemption, the applicant must file Form N-648, Medical Certification for Disability Exemptions. This form must be completed and signed by a doctor.

Sample English and civics tests questions are as follows:

Read the following sentences out loud:

George Washington was the father of our country.

The president lives in the White House.

Answer the following questions out loud:

Who is the president of the United States?

Why are there 50 stars on the American flag?

Choose the best answer to the following questions:

1. How many terms may a president serve?

    a. one

    b. four

    c. two

    d. no limit

2. What country did the Americans fight in the American Revolution?

    a. France

    b. Canada

    c. Germany

    d. England

STRATEGIES TO HELP YOU SUCCEED IN THE INTERVIEW

Many applicants view the interview as the most stressful part of the naturalization process. It doesn't have to be. Here are 10 tips to help you lessen the stress, and handle yourself well.

1. Get to the USCIS office early

   Traffic, bad directions, lack of parking spaces, and long lines for security checkpoints can make you late. Plan ahead; get as much information as possible. Where is the office? What entrance do you use? How long do most people have to wait to get into the building and inside the waiting room? Call ahead, visit the building, and talk with people who are familiar with your local USCIS office. Find out exactly when to leave your house. When you get there early, and know what to expect, you will be better able to relax.

2. Follow directions about the exact paperwork that you need to bring with you

   Bring the documents the USCIS requested, including your permanent resident or alien registration card, your passport (even if expired), and re-entry permits if you have them. If the interview letter asked you to bring other documents, make sure that you have them with you. If you do not bring all of the documents requested by the USCIS, your application could be delayed or denied.

3. Be positive and polite

   A positive attitude tells your interviewer that you are confident—confident in your own abilities and that the naturalization process will go well for you. Shake hands firmly, sit up straight in your chair, and make eye contact. Do not act superior. Treat everyone at the USCIS office with respect, including the person who takes your fingerprints.

4. Bring supporting documents

A copy of your application is useful when you are asked questions about what you answered on it. Other documents can show the USCIS officer that you have a home, have a job, and are active in your community. Bring papers such as the lease for your apartment, a letter from your employer, a copy of your latest pay stub or income tax return, proof of membership in organizations, or a thank-you note for volunteer work.

5. Dress to impress

You do not need to be formal, but a neat and clean appearance shows the USCIS officer that you are serious, and it gives a great first impression.

6. Be prepared for the questions you will be asked

Steps 3 and 4 explain exactly what you need to know and do to pass the English and civics tests. Most people, including American citizens, do not know or remember all of the history and government facts that could be on the test. Spend time studying until you are familiar with all of them. Do all of the practice exercises, including those that help improve your English skills. When you are prepared, you are less nervous and better able to take the tests.

7. Ask for help if you need it

If you do not understand a question from the interviewer or something on a test, politely ask to have it explained to you.

8. Tell the truth

You already know how important it is that everything you say during your interview and everything you write on your application is the truth, but it's worth repeating: If the USCIS finds that something you said or wrote is not true, they can deny your application. If you are already a citizen and they find out about a lie, they can take your citizenship away. Telling the truth is absolutely necessary.

9. Do not make excuses

If there is something on your application that embarrasses you, such as a crime you committed or a divorce, answer any questions about it calmly and directly. Do not offer any new information about the incident unless it is specifically asked for. You may have made a mistake or two in the past, but the interviewer can still get a positive impression if you are likeable and appear to be of good character. Making excuses for past mistakes does not help.

10. Relax

It's not easy to be relaxed, but being prepared, having all the documents you need, looking neat and clean, and being on time can help.

WHAT IF I AM NOT TREATED FAIRLY?

Most USCIS employees are professionals who treat everyone going through the naturalization process with respect. However, if you feel a USCIS employee did not treat you properly, you should speak with his or her direct supervisor. If you cannot speak with that person, write a letter to the director of your district office explaining the situation. The director should be able to resolve the issue.

Another way to make a complaint is by using Form I-847, Report of a Complaint, which can be ordered from the USCIS forms line at 1-800-870-3676. The form is a postcard with the address of USCIS headquarters printed on it.

THE APPLICATION DECISION

Some applicants find out at the end of their interview if they will be granted citizenship. Others must wait for a decision to come in the mail. Either way, the decision is either granted (accepted), continued (put on hold), or denied.

Granted

If your interview goes well and you pass the English and civics tests, you are granted citizenship. Your interviewer may tell you the decision or you may leave the USCIS office without knowing. In the latter case, a notice is sent in the mail telling you of the decision, including when and where your oath ceremony will be. If you find out after your interview, you may be able to take the oath on the same day.

Continued

Your case is continued (put on hold) if you fail the English or civics test (or both), or if you do not bring the correct documents to the interview. If you fail a test, you get a second interview date (typically 60–90 days after the first interview). If you fail again, your application is denied.

If you do not bring the necessary documents, you get Form N-14, which explains the documents you need to provide, and when and how to get those documents to the USCIS. Follow the directions on Form N-14 carefully—if you make a mistake, such as sending the wrong document, sending the right document to the wrong address, or sending the right document too late, your application may be denied.

Denied

The USCIS sends you a letter if your application is denied. In it, they tell you the reason for the denial and explain what you can do if you think the decision to deny is wrong. The notice includes Form N-336, Request for Hearing on a Decision in Naturalization Proceedings under Section 336 of the Act. To ask for a hearing with a USCIS officer, you need to fill out this form and file it within 30 days after you receive the denial letter. A fee (currently $605) is required with Form N-336. Send a check for that amount payable to Department of Homeland Security or U.S. Citizenship and Immigration Services.

After your appeal hearing, you are told whether your application is still denied. If it is, and you still believe your application should be granted, you can file a petition for a new review of your application in U.S. District Court.

THE LOYALTY OATH CEREMONY

If your application is granted, you must attend a loyalty oath ceremony. The ceremony may be held on the day of your interview or you will receive a Notice of Naturalization Oath Ceremony (Form N-445) that tells you the date and time of your ceremony. If you cannot attend the ceremony on the scheduled date, return Form N-445 to your local USCIS office with a letter explaining why you cannot attend and requesting a new date.

On the back of Form N-445 are questions the USCIS officer may ask you before the ceremony about things you may have done since your interview. These questions may include "Have you traveled outside the United States?" and "Have you claimed exemption from military service?" Write your answers to these questions on the back of the form, remembering to answer only about the time since your USCIS interview.

Whether you attend the ceremony on the same day as your interview or on another day, you must first check in with the USCIS and return your permanent resident card. As with your interview, the ceremony is crowded, so you should plan to arrive early. After everyone checks in, an official reads the oath slowly, one part at a time. You are asked to repeat his or her words.

THE OATH OF ALLEGIANCE

I hereby declare, on oath, that I absolutely and entirely renounce and abjure all allegiance and fidelity to any foreign prince, potentate, state, or sovereignty of whom or which I have heretofore been a subject or citizen; that I will support and defend the Constitution and laws of the United States of America against all enemies, foreign and domestic; that I will bear true faith and allegiance to the same; that I will bear arms on behalf of the United States when required by the law; that I will perform noncombatant service in the armed forces of the United States when required by the law; that I will perform work of national importance under civilian direction when required by the law; and that I take this obligation freely without any mental reservation or purpose of evasion; so help me God.

You should note that in the oath you give up allegiance to the country of which you were formerly a citizen. Naturalization requirements also state that you must give up any hereditary title (such as Earl or Baron) or position of nobility you held in that country.

Some parts of the oath may be changed, or modified, for certain individuals. If you cannot say the entire oath for one of the following reasons, write a letter to the USCIS and include it with your application. The USCIS may ask you to bring to the interview or send a document from your religious organization that explains its beliefs and states that you are a member in good standing. If the document is accepted, you can take a modified oath.

The five possible modifications of the oath are:

1. If you would not fight for the United States because of your religious beliefs, you can take the oath without saying "to bear arms on behalf of the United States when required by law."

2. If you would not serve in any way for the Armed Forces because of your religious beliefs, you can take the oath without saying "to perform noncombatant service in the Armed Forces of the United States when required by law."

3. If you cannot swear the oath using the words "on oath," you may say instead "and solemnly affirm."

4. If your religious beliefs prevent you from saying "so help me God," you may leave those words out.

5. If you cannot understand the oath because of a physical or mental disability, you may be excused from the requirement.

After you take the oath, you get a Certificate of Naturalization. This paper is your proof of citizenship. If it is lost, destroyed, or stolen, or if you legally change your name, you need to apply for a replacement. Replacements can take up to one year to receive. During that year, you have no proof of citizenship unless you already have a U.S. passport. For this reason, it makes sense to apply for a passport as soon as you get your Certificate of Naturalization.

Applications for passports are sometimes available at loyalty oath ceremonies, or you can download one online from the U.S. State Department (travel.state.gov/passport/forms/ds11/ds11_842.html), or pick one up at a post office or passport acceptance facility. To find a facility near you where you can get an application and apply for a passport, check online at iafdb.travel.state.gov/ or call the National Passport Information Center (NPIC) at 1-877-487-2778.

CHECKLIST: ARE YOU ELIGIBLE FOR NATURALIZATION?

This guide is designed to help you determine whether you are eligible to apply for and be granted naturalization status or not. It covers the situations of most applicants—those over 18 years of age who have been permanent residents for at least three years. Do not use this guide if you are under 18 years old, are not a permanent resident, and/or have not been a permanent resident for at least three years; you are not eligible to apply for naturalization. (There are a few exceptions for permanent residents 18 years old or over; see the section "Are You Eligible for Citizenship via Naturalization" in Step 1 for more details.)

If you answer all applicable questions and you are not told that your application will be denied, you are probably eligible to apply for naturalization. If you are told your application will be denied for a reason other than length of time in the United States or as a permanent resident, seek the advice of an immigration expert (see the box on pages 9-10 in Step 1 to find out where you can get answers to your questions).

If you are 18 years old or older, and have been a permanent resident for at least five years, answer the following questions:

1. Have you been outside of the United States for 30 months or more?

If you answer "Yes"—Your application will be denied unless those 30 or more months were spent

- serving on board a vessel operated by or registered in the United States;

- working under contract to the U.S. government; or

- performing ministerial or priestly functions for a religious denomination or an interdenominational organization with a valid presence in the United States.

If one of the above exceptions applies to you, continue reading the rest of the questions.

If you answer "No"—Continue reading the rest of the questions to make sure that you are eligible to apply for naturalization.

2. Have you taken a trip outside the United States lasting one year or longer?

If you answer "Yes"—Your application will be denied. The exception to this rule is for those who

- served on board a vessel operated by or registered in the United States;

- worked under contract to the U.S. government; or

- performed ministerial or priestly functions for a religious denomination or an interdenominational organization with a valid presence in the United States.

If you are in one of these categories and you had an approved Form N-470, Application to Preserve Residence for Naturalization Purposes, before leaving the United States for a year or more, you can apply. Continue reading the rest of the questions.

If you answer "No"—Continue reading the rest of the questions to make sure that you are eligible to apply for naturalization.

3. Have you lived in the district or state where you are applying for naturalization for the last three months?

If you answer "Yes"—Continue reading the rest of the questions to make sure that you are eligible to apply for naturalization.

If you answer "No"—You must wait until you have lived there for three months before applying.

4. Can you read, write, and speak basic English? Do you know the history of the United States and its form of government?

If you answer "Yes"—Continue reading the rest of the questions to make sure that you are eligible to apply for naturalization.

If you answer "No"—Your application will be denied unless you meet one of the following exceptions:

- you are over age 50 and have been a permanent resident for at least 20 years;

- you are over age 55 and have been a permanent resident for at least 15 years;

- you are over age 65 and have been a permanent resident for at least 20 years; or

- you have a disability and are filing Form N-648, Medical Certification for Disability Exceptions.

If exceptions 1, 2, or 3 describe you, then you do not have to take the English test. People who meet the requirements for exceptions 1 and 2 must take the civics test in the language of their choice. Those who meet exception 3 must take a simpler version of the civics test in the language of their choice. If exception 4 describes you, you do not have to take the English or civics test.

If you meet one of these four exceptions, continue reading the rest of the questions to make sure that you are eligible to apply for naturalization.

5. Do you have a serious criminal record?

If you answer "Yes"—Your application will be denied.

If you answer "No"—Continue reading the rest of the questions to make sure that you are eligible to apply for naturalization.

6. If you are male, are you registered with the Selective Service?

If you answer "Yes"—Continue reading the rest of the questions to make sure that you are eligible to apply for naturalization.

If you answer "No"—Unless you did not enter the United States before the age of 26, or entered between the ages of 18 and 26 and did not register but have a letter from the Selective Service explaining why, you must be registered or your application will be denied. If you meet these exceptions, continue reading the questions.

7. Have you deserted from the U.S. military?

If you answer "Yes"—Your application will be denied.

If you answer "No"—Continue reading the rest of the questions to make sure that you are eligible to apply for naturalization.

8. Have you received an exemption or discharge from the U.S. military because you are an alien?

> If you answer "Yes"—Your application will be denied.

> If you answer "No"—Continue reading the rest of the questions to make sure that you are eligible to apply for naturalization.

9. Are you willing to serve in the military or civilian service for the United States if the law requires you to do so?

> If you answer "Yes"—Continue reading the rest of the questions to make sure that you are eligible to apply for naturalization.

> If you answer "No "—Unless your religious beliefs or teaching prohibit it, you must be willing to serve or your application will be denied.

10. Will you support the U.S. Constitution?

> If you answer "Yes"—Continue reading the rest of the questions to make sure that you are eligible to apply for naturalization.

> If you answer "No"—Your application will be denied.

11. Do you understand the oath of allegiance to the United States (see page 41), and are you willing to take it?

> If you answer "Yes"—Read the rest of the questions to make sure that you are eligible to apply for naturalization.

> If you answer "No"—Your application will be denied.

If you are 18 years old or older, and have been a permanent resident for three to five years, answer the following three questions:

12. Are you married to and living with a U.S. citizen (who has been a citizen for at least three years)?

13. Have you been married to that citizen for at least three years?

14. Have you remained in the United States for at least 18 months during the past three years?

> If you answer "Yes" to all three questions—Continue reading the rest of the questions to make sure that you are eligible to apply for naturalization.

> If you answer "No" to any of the three questions—Your application will be denied.

15. Did you take a trip out of the United States for longer than six months during the past three years?

> If you answer "Yes"—Your application will be denied.

> If you answer "No"—Continue reading the rest of the questions to make sure that you are eligible to apply for naturalization.

16. Have you lived in the district or state where you are applying for naturalization for the last three months?

> If you answer "Yes"—Continue reading the rest of the questions to make sure that you are eligible to apply for naturalization.

> If you answer "No"—You must wait until you have lived there for three months before applying.

17. Can you read, write, and speak basic English? Do you know the history of the United States and its form of government?

> If you answer "Yes" to both questions—Continue reading the rest of the questions to make sure that you are eligible to apply for naturalization.

> If you answer "No" to either question—Your application will be denied unless you have a disability and are filing Form N-648, Medical Certification for Disability Exceptions.

18. Do you have a serious criminal record?

If you answer "Yes"—Your application will be denied.

If you answer "No"—Continue reading the rest of the questions to make sure that you are eligible to apply for naturalization.

19. If you are male, are you registered with the Selective Service?

If you answer "Yes"—Continue reading the rest of the questions to make sure that you are eligible to apply for naturalization.

If you answer "No"—Unless you did not enter the United States before the age of 26, or entered between the ages of 18 and 26 and did not register but have a letter from the Selective Service explaining why, you must be registered or your application will be denied. If you meet these exceptions, continue reading the questions.

20. Have you deserted from the U.S. military?

If you answer "Yes"—Your application will be denied.

If you answer "No"—Continue reading the rest of the questions to make sure that you are eligible to apply for naturalization.

21. Have you received an exemption or discharge from the U.S. military because you are an alien?

If you answer "Yes"—Your application will be denied.

If you answer "No"—Continue reading the rest of the questions to make sure that you are eligible to apply for naturalization.

22. Are you willing to serve in the military or civilian service for the United States if the law requires you to do so?

If you answer "Yes"—Continue reading the rest of the questions to make sure that you are eligible to apply for naturalization.

If you answer "No"—Unless your religious beliefs or teaching prohibit it, you must be willing to serve or your application will be denied.

23. Will you support the U.S. Constitution?

If you answer "Yes"—Continue reading the rest of the questions to make sure that you are eligible to apply for naturalization.

If you answer "No"—Your application will be denied.

24. Do you understand the oath of allegiance to the United States (see page 41), and are you willing to take it?

If you answer "Yes"—Read the rest of the questions to make sure that you are eligible to apply for naturalization.

If you answer "No"—Your application will be denied.

NOTES

_____

_____

_____

_____

_____

_____

_____

_____

_____

_____

_____

_____

_____

_____

_____

_____

_____

_____

_____

_____

_____

_____

_____

_____

_____

_____

_____

_____

_____

_____

_____

_____

_____

_____

_____

_____

_____

_____

_____

_____

Step 3: **Practicing Reading, Writing, and Speaking English**

To be eligible for citizenship, you must be able to read, write, and speak simple words and phrases in English. This step explains how to improve your English skills and it provides practice exercises similar to those on your test and interview.

HOW YOUR ENGLISH IS TESTED

There are three ways that your English skills are tested: reading, writing, and speaking. To see how well you read English, you are asked to read out loud. You are given one to three simple sentences, and have to read at least one correctly.

To test your writing, you are asked to write one, two, or three simple sentences. To test your speaking ability, during your interview you are asked questions about yourself and your application.

READING AND WRITING VOCABULARY

The USCIS has issued the lists of words that the sentences you need to read and write will contain. To learn them, begin by copying them on a separate sheet of paper. Next to each word, write its definition (look up words you don't know). Then write each word in a sentence. Finally, give the list of writing vocabulary words to someone who can read them to you. Practice writing each word as it is read.

Reading Vocabulary

People: Abraham Lincoln, George Washington

Civics: American flag, Bill of Rights, capital, citizen, city, Congress, country, Father of Our Country, government, president, right, senators, state/states, White House

Places: America, United States, U.S.

Holidays: Presidents' Day, Memorial Day, Flag Day, Independence Day, Labor Day, Columbus Day, Thanksgiving

Question Words: how, what, when, where, who, why

Verbs: can, come, do/does, elects, have/has, is/are/was/be, lives/lived, meet, name, pay, vote, want

Other: a, for, here, in, of, on, the, to, we, colors, dollar bill, first, largest, many, most, north, one, people, second, south

Writing Vocabulary

People: Adams, Lincoln, Washington

Civics: American Indians, capital, citizens, Civil War, Congress, Father of Our Country, flag, free, freedom of speech, president, right, senators, state/states, White House

Places: Alaska, California, Canada, Delaware, Mexico, New York City, Washington, Washington, D.C., United States

Months: February, May, June, July, September, October, November

Holidays: Presidents' Day, Memorial Day, Flag Day, Independence Day, Labor Day, Columbus Day, Thanksgiving

Verbs: can, come, elect, have/has, is/was/be, lives/lived, meets, pay, vote, want

Other: and, during, for, here, in, of, on, the, to, we, blue, dollar bill, fifty/50, first, largest, most, north, one, one hundred/100, people, red, second, south, taxes, white

FIVE WAYS TO IMPROVE YOUR ENGLISH SKILLS

The following five things will help improve your English skills:

1. Reading the newspaper

2. Writing your personal history

3. Reading out loud

4. Listening

5. Talking with people

Reading the Newspaper

Improving your English skills means not only practicing what you already know, but also learning more. A great way to learn new words and better understand grammar is to read the newspaper every day.

Choose a national newspaper rather than a smaller local one. Then, spend at least 20 minutes reading. As you read, write down the words you do not know. When you are finished, look up the words in a dictionary, and write the definition next to the word. Pick three of the words and write them on smaller pieces of paper or cards that you can carry with you. Check the cards a few times a day, and try using the words in a conversation.

For more practice, choose the story that had the most words you did not know in it, and read it out loud.

Writing Your Personal History

Form N-400 asks many questions about your life and experiences, and during your interview, you may be asked questions about the information you wrote on that form. This exercise helps you with the form and the interview, and it improves your English skills too.

Tell your story, in English, by writing or typing it. Imagine someone has asked you about your life: Where are you from? What was it like there? Who are your family members? What are some happy memories? Have you traveled to other countries? Why do you want to become a U.S. citizen? Include your family history, children, and a description of the jobs you have held. Try to write a page or more about your life.

Reading Out Loud

Reading out loud, whether to yourself or another person, improves your confidence with spoken English. Try to read at least two stories or articles in front of a mirror for about 15 minutes each day. They could be stories from the newspaper, magazine articles, or pages from a book.

If you can record your voice while you are reading, you can play the recording back to hear how you are improving. The more you practice, the better you get at reading out loud.

Listening

Understanding spoken English is harder for some people than writing or reading. Conversations in stores and on the street can be difficult—people may talk quickly, have an accent that is hard to figure out, or use words you don't understand. The best way to improve your listening skills is to practice in a quiet place where there are no distractions. When you listen to the television, radio, or a book on tape, you can concentrate on what is being said. Some televisions even have "closed captioning," meaning they can print out what is being said at the bottom of the screen. Reading these captions while you listen can help you make sure you understand the conversation.

Talking with People

Talking with people is another great way to improve your English skills, but you need good listening skills at the same time. If the people you are talking with are hard to understand, stop them and let them know. They can slow down, or use different words to say the same thing. Talking with people forces you to use English instead of just studying it. Many people find that talking not only improves their English skills, but also helps them to understand better what other people are saying.

PRACTICE EXERCISES

Follow the instructions to complete the exercises, which were written to help you improve and study your English skills.

Important Terms to Define

These words are all found on Form N-400, the Application for Naturalization. Your interviewer may ask you questions about them to see if you understand the application. If you know the word, simply write its definition in the space provided. If you are not sure of a word's meaning, look it up in the dictionary or in this book and then copy the definition in the space provided.

1. allegiance _____

_____

_____

2. Constitution _____

_____

_____

3. citizen _____

_____

_____

4. Form N-400 _____

_____

_____

5. U.S. Citizenship and Immigration Services (USCIS) _____

_____

_____

6. interview _____

_____

_____

7. immigrant _____

_____

_____

8. continuous residence _____

_____

_____

9. moral character _____

_____

_____

10. naturalization _____

_____

_____

11. naturalization oath ceremony _____

_____

_____

12. fingerprint _____

_____

_____

13. oath _____

_____

_____

14. passport _____

_____

_____

15. permanent resident _____

_____

_____

Civics Questions

These are the kinds of questions you may be asked during your interview. They are about history and government, which is explained in Step 4. If you can't answer one or more of the questions, check the answers on page in this book, and test yourself again when you have completed Step 6.

1. What is one right of citizens only? _____

_____

_____

2. What are the two major political parties? _____

_____

_____

3. Who signs bills into laws? _____

_____

_____

4. How long is a senator's term? _____

_____

_____

5. What is one branch of the government? _____

_____

_____

6. What is the Bill of Rights? _____

_____

_____

7. What is one responsibility of citizenship? _____

_____

_____

8. Who fought the Civil War? _____

_____

_____

9. What was the Emancipation Proclamation? _____

_____

_____

10. How old do you have to be before you can vote? _____

_____

_____

Reading Comprehension

These questions help you practice reading and writing in English. Read each passage and answer the questions that follow. All of the answers may be found in the passages.

Passage 1:

The United States government is made up of three branches. These branches are described in the Constitution. The first is the executive branch, which includes the president, the vice president, and the cabinet. The executive branch signs bills into law, commands the United States military, and negotiates with leaders from other countries. The legislative branch is led by the House of Representatives and the Senate, which together are called Congress. Congress makes laws and has the power to declare war. The judicial branch is led by the Supreme Court, and includes the entire court system of the United States. The nine justices on the Supreme Court are appointed by the president for lifetime terms. They interpret the Constitution, and their decisions cannot be overturned by any other court.

1. Who appoints Supreme Court justices? _____

_____

_____

2. What two bodies make up Congress? _____

_____

3. The president's cabinet is in which branch? _____

_____

_____

4. Who has the power to declare war? _____

_____

_____

5. How long is the term of a Supreme Court justice? _____

_____

_____

Passage 2:

America is known as a melting pot because it is made up of citizens who came from many countries to have a better life. Immigrants left their countries because of different reasons. Some came to America because they needed to find work, and others came to escape from war. For many years, immigrants came to America by passing the Statue of Liberty, which was a gift of friendship from France, and landing on Ellis Island in the New York Harbor. Twelve million immigrants passed through Ellis Island from 1892 until it closed in 1954.

6. Where is Ellis Island? _____

_____

_____

7. How many immigrants passed through Ellis Island? _____

_____

_____

8. Immigrants come to America for many reasons—name one. _____

_____

_____

9. Where did the Statue of Liberty come from? _____

_____

_____

10. Why is America called a melting pot? _____

_____

_____

Reading Out Loud

During your citizenship test you must read 10 sentences out loud. The sentences are very similar to the following ones. Practice reading them out loud to yourself, a family member, or a friend.

1. I live in America.

2. Independence Day is in July.

3. George Washington is on the dollar bill.

4. Many people elect the president.

5. Where is the White House?

6. Congress is in the capital.

7. Come to the largest country.

8. Abraham Lincoln was a senator.

9. How do we elect senators?

10. Citizens elect the president.

ANSWERS AND EXPLANATIONS

Here are the answers and explanations for the practice questions. For more practice, see the practice test in Step 6.

Important Terms to Define

1. Allegiance is loyalty to a nation. When you say the Pledge of Allegiance, you promise to be loyal to the United States.

2. The Constitution is the supreme law of the land. It explains our laws, our government, and the powers of the government.

3. A citizen is someone who by birth or naturalization owes loyalty to a country and is protected by it.

4. Form N-400 is the Application for Naturalization.

5. The USCIS is the government agency that helps immigrants become citizens.

6. After you file Form N-400, you get an appointment for an interview. In the interview, you meet with someone from the USCIS to go over your application and take the English and civics tests.

7. An immigrant is someone who leaves one country to live in another.

8. Continuous residence refers to the length of time a permanent resident lives in the United States without taking a long trip out of the country. Most people who apply for naturalization need five years of continuous residence.

9. Moral character refers to the kind of person you are. To be eligible for citizenship, you must be of good moral character. If you committed a certain type of crime, you may not be eligible to become a citizen.

10. Naturalization is the way an immigrant becomes a citizen of the United States.

11. During the naturalization oath ceremony you take the oath of allegiance and become a U.S. citizen.

12. A fingerprint is an impression of your fingertip. Fingerprints are taken after you file the Application for Naturalization. They are used for identification because no two people's fingerprints are alike.

13. An oath is a promise. When you say the oath of allegiance to the United States, you promise to renounce foreign allegiances, support the Constitution, and serve the United States.

14. A passport is a government document that proves citizenship and allows you to travel to other countries.

15. A permanent resident is someone who has permanent resident status according to immigration law. He or she has a permanent resident card. After five years, a permanent resident can apply for naturalization.

Civics Question Responses

1. Only citizens can vote in federal elections and run for federal office.

2. The two major political parties are Democratic and Republican.

3. The president signs bills into laws.

4. Senators are elected to six-year terms.

5. One branch of the government is (any of the following are correct) legislative, executive, judicial.

6. The Bill of Rights is the first 10 amendments to the Constitution.

7. The responsibilities of citizenship include voting in federal elections and serving on a jury if called.

8. The Civil War was fought by Northern free states against Southern slave-holding states.

9. The Emancipation Proclamation was an order issued by President Lincoln that freed the slaves.

10. You must be at least 18 to vote for president.

Reading Comprehension

1. The president appoints Supreme Court justices.

2. Congress is made up of the House of Representatives and the Senate.

3. The president's cabinet is part of the executive branch.

4. Congress has the power to declare war.

5. Supreme Court justices serve lifetime terms.

6. Ellis Island is in New York Harbor.

7. Twelve million immigrants passed through Ellis Island.

8. Immigrants came to America to find work; they also came to escape war.

9. The Statue of Liberty came from France.

10. America is called a melting pot because it is made up of people from many different countries.

NOTES

_____

_____

_____

_____

_____

_____

_____

_____

_____

_____

_____

_____

_____

_____

_____

_____

_____

_____

_____

_____

_____

_____

_____

_____

_____

_____

_____

_____

_____

_____

_____

_____

_____

_____

_____

_____

_____

_____

_____

_____

_____

_____

_____

_____

_____

_____

_____

_____

_____

_____

_____

_____

_____

_____

_____

_____

_____

_____

_____

_____

_____

_____

_____

Step 4: **Learning about U.S. History and Government**

During your interview with the USCIS, your knowledge of U.S. history is tested, along with your knowledge about how the government works. This portion of the interview is known as the civics test. The interviewer asks you to answer a set of questions on history and government out loud, or to take a written multiple-choice test. The test includes up to 20 questions.

In this part of Step 4, you learn everything you need to know about history to pass that test. Later on in the step, you review the basics of government.

THE COLONIAL PERIOD

During the colonial period, settlers from Europe came to America and formed a new country.

Important Terms and Names

Native Americans	Revolutionary War
colonists	Declaration of Independence
Jamestown	George Washington
Mayflower	Thomas Jefferson
slavery	13 colonies

Native Population

Before Europeans came to what is now called North America, millions of Native Americans lived in the so-called "New World." Although it is not known how many distinct tribes or nations of Native Americans were here, early European settlers said they met approximately 60 tribes just in the land east of the Mississippi River. These tribes had their own languages, styles of clothing and shelter, and methods of hunting, growing, and preparing food. Because of these differences, and the fact that the tribes were geographically separated from one another, it was impossible for these native people to join together and successfully negotiate with and protect themselves from the Europeans who began exploring North America in the 1400s.

Native Americans Today

There are 22 tribes of Native Americans that are recognized by the United States government. They are Cherokee, Navajo, Sioux, Chippewa, Choctaw, Pueblo, Apache, Iroquois, Creek, Blackfeet, Seminole, Cheyenne, Arawak, Shawnee, Mohegan, Huron, Oneida, Lakota, Crow, Teton, Hopi, and Inuit.

European Explorers

During the 1400s and 1500s, many of the kings and queens of Europe sent men across the oceans to find gold and claim land. Explorers from Spain, England, and France came to North America during this time. The Spanish claimed much of the land, and its riches, that stretched from what is now California, south to Argentina, and east to Florida. The French took parts of Canada and upper northeastern North America. The English claimed much of the East Coast.

The Colonists

King James II of Britain sent ships full of settlers to the New World. The first successful British colony was established in Jamestown (named for the king) by the Virginia Company. In 1620, the *Mayflower* sailed from Britain to Plymouth, where its passengers established the Massachusetts Bay Colony. These colonists were Protestants who were not allowed to practice their religion freely under their Catholic king. It was important to them that in their new land they be able to have the freedom to practice their religion without being persecuted by their leaders. They were also looking for economic opportunity.

Over the next hundred years, more colonies grew along the East Coast from New Hampshire to Georgia, bringing the total to 13. Those colonies were:

Connecticut	New York
Delaware	North Carolina
Georgia	Pennsylvania
Maryland	Rhode Island
Massachusetts	South Carolina
New Hampshire	Virginia
New Jersey	

The Rise of Slavery

In 1619, the first Africans arrived in Jamestown. They had been captured in Africa, and brought to be slaves. By 1660, there were hundreds of thousands of Africans in America, most in the southern colonies. They could be bought and sold, and had no legal status or rights. By the start of the American Revolution a hundred years later, there were about four million slaves in the United States.

Anger toward England

Although the colonists first came to America looking for freedom, England kept firm control over them. The colonists were not allowed to rule themselves, and had to pay many taxes to the king. The English collected tax money from the colonists for paper, sugar, tea, and many other items. The stamp tax, for example, had to be paid for every printed piece of paper used by the colonists. The colonists reacted by joining together to fight the taxes. Many stopped buying English products, including a shipment of tea that arrived in the Boston harbor. The colonists boarded the ship and dumped the tea into the water in what was known as the Boston Tea Party. England responded by closing the harbor and passing even more laws to control the colonists.

In 1774, representatives from 12 of the 13 colonies traveled to Philadelphia to organize a protest against England. They called themselves the Continental Congress, and came up with a list of demands, including stopping the collection of many taxes.

The Revolutionary War Breaks Out

The British king was not interested in meeting the colonists' demands. A group of colonists collected weapons and organized a group of soldiers known as Minutemen. When the Minutemen found out that British soldiers were coming to arrest them and take their weapons, they fought back. The Revolutionary War began with the "shot heard 'round the world," fired by the Minutemen at the soldiers. Word spread throughout the colonies, and many more colonists joined the fight. George Washington was named general of the growing Continental Army. As the fighting continued, the Continental Congress met again, and decided that they wanted independence from Britain.

The Declaration of Independence

Five members of the Continental Congress, led by Thomas Jefferson, wrote a document to explain to Britain that the colonies wanted their independence. The document in fact said that the colonies were free. It was adopted on July 4, 1776, and was called the Declaration of Independence. In it, Jefferson wrote that it was within the colonists' rights to be independent, and listed the things that Britain did to make them want to form their own government (such as collecting taxes and forcing colonists to take in British soldiers). Jefferson stated that "all men are created equal," and they have the right to "life, liberty, and the pursuit of happiness."

THE 4TH OF JULY

Americans celebrate Independence Day on July 4 each year to commemorate the signing of the Declaration of Independence.

THE FLAG OF THE UNITED STATES

The Continental Congress passed the first Flag Act in 1777, which said that the U.S. flag would be made of 13 alternating red and white stripes, with 13 white stars on a blue background. The number 13 represented the original 13 states (see Figure 4.1). As new states became part of the country, stars were added for each, and the stars were eventually placed in rows. Although there are now 50 stars, representing the 50 states, there are still 13 stripes representing the original 13 states (see Figure 4.2).

Figure 4.1   The First U.S. Flag

Figure 4.2   The Current U.S. Flag

Practice Questions

1. Why did the colonists come to America? _____

   _____

   _____

2. Name one of the Native American tribes in the United States today.

   _____

   _____

3. Slaves were owned for life and had no legal _____.

4. Name four of the original 13 colonies.

   _____

   _____

5. The main writer of the Declaration of Independence was

   _____.

6. The Declaration of Independence was adopted on _____

7. Independence Day is celebrated every year on _____.

8. Name two rights in the Declaration of Independence. _____

   _____.

9. When the colonists came to America, they found _____
   already living here.

10. The 13 stripes on the flag represent _____

   _____.

Answers and Explanations

1. The colonists came to have religious and political freedom and economic opportunity.

   Explanation: Colonists came to America in large part because they were not allowed to practice their religion without fear of persecution. They wanted to live where they could be free to believe what they chose and where they would have economic opportunity.

2. Any one of the following is correct: Cherokee, Navajo, Sioux, Chippewa, Choctaw, Pueblo, Apache, Iroquois, Creek, Blackfeet, Seminole, Cheyenne, Arawak, Shawnee, Mohegan, Huron, Oneida, Lakota, Crow, Teton, Hopi, Inuit.

3. rights

4. Any four of the following are correct: New Hampshire, Massachusetts, Rhode Island, Connecticut, New York, New Jersey, Pennsylvania, Delaware, Maryland, Virginia, North Carolina, South Carolina, and Georgia.

   Explanation: The first settlements were established in Plymouth and Jamestown. Over many years, the settlements grew into colonies, and some people left to start new colonies. By the mid-1700s, there were 13 English colonies along the east coast of what is now the United States.

5. Thomas Jefferson

6. July 4, 1776

   Explanation: The Declaration of Independence was adopted by the Continental Congress after three days of making changes to Jefferson's original.

7. July 4

   Explanation: We celebrate Independence Day on July 4 to commemorate the signing of the Declaration of Independence.

8. Life, liberty, and/or the pursuit of happiness

   Explanation: Thomas Jefferson wrote in the Declaration of Independence that these three rights belonged to every man.

9. Native Americans or American Indians

Explanation: There were millions of Native Americans living here when the colonists arrived.

10. the 13 original colonies

Explanation: The flag began with 13 stripes and 13 stars. Every time a state was added, a star was added, but the number of stripes stayed the same.

FROM THE U.S. CONSTITUTION TO THE CIVIL WAR

The writing of the Constitution and beginning years of independence were not easy. America fought two wars during this time, and had to deal with the difficult issue of slavery.

Important Terms and Names

Constitution	Louisiana Territory
Constitutional Convention	War of 1812
supreme law of the land	"Star-Spangled Banner"
George Washington	Mexican-American War
Washington, D.C.	Abraham Lincoln
Benjamin Franklin	Civil War
Federalist Papers	war between the states
John Jay	Emancipation Proclamation
Alexander Hamilton	Spanish-American War
James Madison	Susan B. Anthony
Publius	Statue of Liberty

The Constitution

Once the United States of America was established, leaders from each state met to decide on laws and a form of government. They began writing the Constitution, which became the supreme law of the land in 1789, almost 13 years after the Declaration of Independence was ratified. The Constitution established the court system, the Congress, and the presidency, including an explanation of how to select the president and the qualifications needed for the position.

Soon after the Constitution became law, George Washington was elected as president of the United States, which also meant he was the first commander in chief of the U.S. military. Because he was the first president, Washington had to decide how to use the power of his office. He set up the first cabinet, or group of advisors, toured different areas of the country, and helped establish the country's financial system.

Washington's success as the first president resulted in his nickname, "Father of Our Country." He was president for nine years, followed by John Adams, who served four years.

A REMARKABLE FOUNDING FATHER ─────────

The oldest member of the Constitutional Convention, and also
a signer of the Declaration of Independence, was Benjamin
Franklin. Franklin was a talented man whose contributions to the
United States were many. He wrote and published *Poor Richard's
Almanack*, started the first free library, and served as the first
Postmaster general. After signing the Declaration of Independence,
Franklin went to France as a diplomat.

Westward Expansion

Thomas Jefferson was elected the third president in 1801. A year into Jefferson's
presidency, he negotiated a deal with Napoleon Bonaparte to buy the Louisiana
Territory from France. Known as the Louisiana Purchase (see Figure 4.3), this deal
doubled the size of the United States. In order to encourage people to leave eastern
states for the new territory, government land was sold very cheaply to those who in
return promised to work that land.

Figure 4.3   The Louisiana Purchase

War of 1812

Thirty years after granting independence to the United States, England was still
trying to control the new country. It captured more than 10,000 American sailors on
oceans around the world, and provided weapons to Native Americans in the west
so they could fight against settlers. England also had a large army in Canada.

In 1812, President Madison declared the Second War of Independence, now known as the War of 1812. British troops invaded the United States, took over many forts, burned Washington, D.C. and attempted to take Baltimore Harbor. The war ended in 1814, after the Americans won the Battle of New Orleans and both countries signed a peace treaty.

THE NATIONAL ANTHEM

In 1814, Francis Scott Key visited the British fleet in Chesapeake Bay, Virginia, to ask them to release a prisoner taken after the burning of Washington, D.C. Key was held on a ship overnight as the British tried to take Fort McHenry. When he woke the next day, he saw the American flag still flying over the fort. His happiness inspired him to write a poem about the event. The poem was set to music, and "The Star-Spangled Banner" became the official national anthem in 1931.

Tension Between the North and the South

Although Congress stopped the slave trade in 1808, Southern states were allowed to keep the slaves they already owned. Southern farmers grew cotton, sugar, and tobacco—all crops that were in great demand and that needed much labor to get from the field to the market. They had to be picked carefully by hand, which took time.

As America added new areas in the South and West, Southern farmers were able to farm even more land, and slave labor was used. They made huge profits because they did not have to pay their workers.

However, in the Northern states—known as Free States—owning slaves was against the law. As new states were added to the Union, Northerners wanted them to be free, and Southerners argued that they should be slave states. Some Northerners began speaking out against slavery, and wanted it to be illegal in every state. The number of slaves doubled during this time, growing from two to four million by 1860.

The Civil War

IIn 1861, Abraham Lincoln became president. He was against slavery. The Southern slave-holding states worried that he would make slavery illegal. Their economy depended on the free labor of slaves, and they wanted to make sure that their rights as states allowed them to make their own laws so they could keep their slaves. Seven Southern states declared that they were no longer part of the United States. A month after Lincoln took office, Southerners shot at federal troops in South Carolina, and the Civil War, or the War Between the States, began. Four more states declared that they were leaving the Union, and 11 Southern states formed the Confederate States of America.

During the war, President Lincoln issued the Emancipation Proclamation, which freed all slaves in the 11 confederate states. It also allowed African Americans to join the Union army. After four years, the Civil War ended, bringing the Confederate states back into the Union. Lincoln only enjoyed the victory for a short time—he was assassinated one week after the war ended.

A REMARKABLE WOMAN

Susan B. Anthony began speaking out for the rights of women and of slaves in the 1850s. After the Civil War, when former male slaves were given the right to vote, Anthony demanded that women be given this right too. She spent the rest of her life fighting for women's rights, but she died before women got the right to vote in 1920.

Spanish-American War

The 1800s saw the United States fight in four wars. The fourth, the Spanish-American War, was in 1898, and began with America's support of the Cuban people, who were fighting for their independence against Spain. The United States sent one of its battleships, the USS *Maine*, to Cuba, where it exploded and sank. The United States demanded that Spain give up control of Cuba, and Spain declared war against the United States.

For about three months, the Spanish fought to keep control of Cuba, Puerto Rico, Guam, and the Philippines. They lost to the United States, which claimed all of those territories.

SYMBOL OF FREEDOM

In 1885, The French gave the Statue of Liberty to the United States to celebrate the centennial, or hundred years since the founding of our country. The Statue was placed on a 12-mile island, known as Liberty Island, off the coast of New Jersey in New York Harbor in the Hudson River, where it remains today.

Practice Questions

1. When the Founding Fathers attended the Constitutional Convention, what did they do?

   _____

   _____

2. The Constitution was written in _____.

3. The Constitution is known as the "supreme law of the land" because

   _____

4. Who is the "Father of our Country"? _____

5. Name one thing Benjamin Franklin is famous for. _____

   _____

6. The first president was _____.

7. Name one writer of the Federalist Papers. _____

8. What is the capital of the United States? _____

9. What does the president's cabinet do? _____

   _____

10. Who is commander in chief of the United States military? _____

    _____

11. In 1803, the United States purchased _____ from France.

12. What is the National Anthem of the United States? _____

13. The war between Northern and Southern states was called _____

_____.

14. Why did the Southern states want to own slaves? _____

_____

15. Many factors led to the Civil War. One of those was _____

16. Name one important thing accomplished by President Lincoln. _____

_____.

17. What did the Emancipation Proclamation do? _____

_____

18. One of the wars fought by the United States in the 1800s was _____

_____.

19. What is Susan B. Anthony known for? _____

20. Where is the Statue of Liberty? _____

Answers and Explanations

1. wrote the Constitution

   Explanation: The Constitutional Convention, or Philadelphia Convention, was a gathering of 55 delegates from several states. The delegates are known as the Founding Fathers.

2. 1787

   Explanation: It took the Founding Fathers four months to work out compromises and come up with a Constitution that everyone agreed on.

3. no other law can take its place

   Explanation: The federal and state governments cannot pass laws that take the place of the Constitution.

4. George Washington

   Explanation: George Washington was given the nickname "Father of Our Country" because he was the first president.

5. Any one of the following is correct: oldest delegate to the Constitutional Convention, writer of *Poor Richard's Almanack*, started the first free library, served as a U.S. diplomat, was the first postmaster general.

   Explanation: Benjamin Franklin was one of the Founding Fathers whose contributions to his country are many.

6. George Washington

   Explanation: Washington was chosen unanimously by the delegates of the Constitutional Convention to be our first president in 1787.

7. Any one of the following is correct: Publius, John Jay, Alexander Hamilton, James Madison.

   Explanation: All of the essays making up the Federalist Papers were signed "Publius," but most people believe they were written by Madison, Hamilton, and Jay.

8. Washington, D.C.

Explanation: Washington, D.C. has been the capital of the United States since 1791.

9. advises the president

Explanation: The president chooses his advisors, who together are called his cabinet. Congress must approve the cabinet members.

10. the president

Explanation: The Constitution gives the title Commander in Chief of the Army, Navy, and Militias to the president.

11. Louisiana, or the Louisiana Territory

Explanation: President Thomas Jefferson bought the Louisiana Territory, doubling the size of the country, and making westward expansion possible.

12. The National Anthem is the "Star-Spangled Banner".

Explanation: Written during the war of 1812 by Francis Scott Key, the "Star-Spangled Banner" is a patriotic song about the American flag and America's victory over and freedom from its enemies.

13. the Civil War, or War Between the States

Explanation: The Civil War divided the country between Northern states and Southern states that broke away from the United States and formed the Confederacy.

14. because they provided free labor to get the crops grown by Southern farmers from the field to the market; they made huge profits for Southern farmers

Explanation: Slaves were not paid like workers in the North, so Southern farmers got to keep all of the money they made selling their crops.

15. Any one of the following is correct: slavery, states' rights, economic reasons.

Explanation: Southern states wanted to keep their slaves and Northern states wanted to free them. The economy in the South depended on slaves, who had to work without being paid. The Southern states also wanted to protect their right to make their own laws in case the federal government made slavery illegal.

16. freed the slaves (Emancipation Proclamation), saved the Union (kept the country from being divided), was our leader during the Civil War.

    Explanation: Abraham Lincoln was one of the United States' greatest presidents. He served during the Civil War, and is given credit for keeping the country together when Southern states tried to form their own union (called the Confederacy). At the end of the war, he signed the Emancipation Proclamation, which freed the slaves.

17. freed the slaves

    Explanation: Signed by Abraham Lincoln in 1863, the Emancipation Proclamation freed the slaves, who were being held in Southern, or Confederate, states.

18. Any of the following is correct: War of 1812, Mexican-American War, Civil War, Spanish-American War

    Explanation: More Americans lost their lives fighting wars in the 1800s than in the five wars the United States fought in the 1900s.

19. fighting for civil rights or the rights of women

    Explanation: Susan B. Anthony spent most of her life trying to get the same rights for all Americans, black or white, male or female.

20. Any one of the following is correct: New York (Harbor), Liberty Island, New Jersey, near New York City, on the Hudson (River).

    Explanation: The Statue of Liberty was a gift to the United States from France. When it arrived in 1885 it was placed on a 12-acre island in New York Harbor.

FROM RECONSTRUCTION TO WORLD WAR I

After the Civil War, America grew as people from many countries came to make better lives for themselves and their families. At the beginning of the 20th century, the nation came together to fight in World War I.

Important Terms and Names

Reconstruction	Ellis Island
Andrew Johnson	World War I
Civil Rights Amendment	Allies
immigration	President Wilson
melting pot	League of Nations

Reconstruction

After Lincoln's death, following the rules of the Constitution, his vice president, Andrew Johnson, became president. Johnson had to bring the country together again, or "reconstruct" it, after the Civil War. During Reconstruction, the Confederate states came back to the Union, and the Constitution was changed to make slavery illegal. In response, most of the Southern states passed laws that made it very difficult for slaves to be free. The Congress passed the Fourteenth Amendment, known as the Civil Rights Amendment, and the Fifteenth Amendment to give African Americans full citizenship and the right to vote.

Nonetheless, laws did not change the way Southerners felt and acted; most simply ignored the new laws, while others became angry and violent toward freed slaves. They were also angry with the president and Congress, who they believed were forcing a new way of life on them. Life for African Americans in the South was in many ways as bad as it was when they were slaves.

Immigration

The United States is often referred to as a "melting pot," a place where people from many other countries, for many reasons, come to live. These people bring with them their cultures, languages, and customs, and come together to form one nation. The original colonies were settled by English immigrants seeking religious freedom. By the time they founded the United States, other English immigrants, such as the Quakers, were joined by thousands from Germany and Ireland, along with hundreds of thousands of Africans brought to America by force in the slave trade.

Because of famines in Ireland, millions of Irish immigrants arrived in the 1800s. Poverty and the wish to practice their religion freely brought millions of Swedes and Norwegians here at the same time. Persecution was the reason about two million European Jews came to America beginning in 1880, and poverty caused the same number of Italians to seek a better life in America.

ELLIS ISLAND

Immigrants from Europe came on ships that landed in the New York harbor. During the late 1800s and early 1900s, there were so many people arriving each day that an immigration station was opened on Ellis Island to handle them. To get to Ellis Island, the ships had to pass the Statue of Liberty, which became a symbol of welcome to the country (see Figure 4.4). During the 62 years it was open, 12 million immigrants landed on Ellis Island before they were allowed to enter America.

Figure 4.4   The Statue of Liberty

World War I

In 1914, war broke out in Europe. The United States, under President Woodrow Wilson, tried to get England and Germany to agree to a peace treaty after three years of fighting, but was not successful. America stayed neutral, taking neither side, until German submarines destroyed American ships in the Atlantic Ocean. President Wilson declared war against Germany in 1917. The United States joined the Allies (countries who were already fighting Germany together), which included England, France, Russia, and Italy. The war ended in 1918 when a peace treaty was signed in Paris.

When the treaty was signed, President Wilson suggested that all of the countries that had been in the war form the League of Nations, a group that would help countries settle their differences so they could prevent another World War.

Practice Questions

1. The period after the Civil War, when the Confederate States came back into the Union, is known as _____.

2. List three of the reasons why people immigrated to the United States.

   _____

   _____

   _____

3. The statue in New York that welcomed immigrants is called

   _____.

4. Alongside which countries did America fight during World War I?

   _____

5. The first immigration station that millions of immigrants arrived at was

   _____.

6. When Lincoln died, his _____,

   Andrew Johnson, became president.

7. In World War I, who was America's enemy? _____

   _____

8. During Reconstruction, the Constitution was changed to make _____

   _____ illegal.

9. Which president had the idea for the League of Nations?

_____

10. Because it is made up of people from many different cultures and countries, the United States is sometimes called a _____

_____.

Answers and Explanations

1. The period after the Civil War, when the Confederate states came back into the Union, was called Reconstruction.

2. Some of the reasons people immigrated to the United States included seeking religious freedom and escaping from famines, wars, persecution, and poverty.

   Explanation: Most Americans are the descendants of immigrants, who came to this country because they believed they would have a better life here.

3. The Statue of Liberty welcomed immigrants in New York.

4. The Americans joined the Allies, France, Russia, England, and Italy, in World War I.

   Explanation: Because Germany's attack on American ships brought the United States into the war, the United States joined the group of allies that was fighting Germany.

5. Millions of immigrants landed on Ellis Island before they were allowed into America.

   Explanation: Because so many immigrants were arriving daily in the late 1800s, an immigration station was built where they could be processed. On Ellis Island, the immigrants were checked to make sure they had no legal or medical problems before they were allowed into the country.

6. After Lincoln died, Vice President Andrew Johnson became president.

7. Germany was America's enemy during World War I.

   Explanation: The United States did not want to get involved in the war in Europe, and had no reason to do so until German submarines began attacking American ships in the Atlantic Ocean. Congress declared war on Germany in 1917.

8. The Constitution was changed to make slavery illegal during Reconstruction.

9. Woodrow Wilson first came up with the idea for the League of Nations.

   Explanation: After the First World War, President Wilson wanted to ensure that the world would never be at war again. He proposed that all of the countries that had been involved in the war form a group called the League of Nations that would work to negotiate and settle differences between its members.

10. A "melting pot" refers to a place that is made up of people from different cultures and backgrounds.

FROM THE AFTERMATH OF WORLD WAR I TO THE PRESENT

During the 20th century, America continued to change. People demanded equal rights for all, no matter whether they were male or female, black or white. The Great Depression created widespread poverty, but also sparked important changes in the government. The United States was also involved in conflicts with other nations, including World War II and the Cold War.

Important Terms and Names

Great Depression	President Eisenhower
Franklin Roosevelt	segregation
New Deal	John F. Kennedy
Nineteenth Amendment	Dr. Martin Luther King Jr.
World War II	September 11, 2001

Great Depression

In 1929, the stock market "crashed," meaning that its value dropped very quickly. Businesses, factories, and banks closed, leaving many people without work or savings. By 1932, one out of every four Americans was jobless, and poverty was widespread.

In 1933, Franklin Roosevelt became president, and promised to bring America out of the Depression. He introduced many government programs, together called the New Deal, which would help the country to recover. The New Deal created jobs, helped banks and businesses reopen, and started Social Security.

WOMEN'S RIGHTS

African Americans were not the only group in the United States fighting for their rights. Women were not allowed to vote in most states until 1920, when the Nineteenth Amendment, which gave them that right, was added to the Constitution. The amendment was a victory for the thousands of American women who were a part of the suffrage movement, working to make sure that all citizens—men and women—were given the right to vote.

World War II

In 1939, war broke out in Europe when Germany took Poland, invaded France, and began bombing England. Under Adolf Hitler, the German army attacked other countries all over Europe, and moved into Russia and Africa.

The United States did not want to get involved in another war, and initially stayed out of the conflict. However, in 1941, the Japanese bombed the U.S. Navy base in Pearl Harbor, Hawaii, destroying five ships and 180 planes, and killing over 2,300 Americans. Congress declared war on Japan the next day. Japan's allies, Germany and Italy, declared war on the United States a few days later.

World War II was fought in Europe and in the Pacific, where Japan was invading China, Singapore, and other countries. The United States had armies in both places, and was an ally of England, France, and Russia. After four years of fighting, Italy surrendered in 1943; Germany surrendered two years later. World War II did not end until later in 1945, when Japan surrendered after the United States dropped atomic bombs on two of its cities.

After the war, the countries that had fought in it realized that the League of Nations, which was formed after World War I, did not fulfill its purpose of preventing another conflict. A new organization was proposed to take its place and do a better job of keeping peace. It was called the United Nations, a term used a few years earlier by President Roosevelt to describe the allies who were fighting in World War II. Fifty-one countries were members of the United Nations when it was created in 1945.

FROM GENERAL TO PRESIDENT

Dwight Eisenhower served in the United States Army from the time he graduated from the military academy through the Cold War. After the Japanese bombed Pearl Harbor, he was made commanding general. By 1944, he was supreme commander and led American forces to victory in World War II. He returned home a hero, and began a career in politics. He served two terms as president, from 1953-61

The Cold War

After World War II, Russia took over many neighboring countries and incorporated them into the Soviet Union. The line between most of Europe and the Soviet

Union was called the Iron Curtain. President Truman and England's Prime Minister Winston Churchill worked together to try to keep the Soviet Union from threatening any other countries. The United States and the Soviet Union began making nuclear weapons, weapons much more powerful than the atomic bombs of World War II. They were in an "arms race" to see who could have the most, and most powerful weapons. The Cold War got its name from the fact that because the weapons were so powerful, both countries were afraid to use them, and therefore never fought each other directly.

One of the countries taken over by the Soviet Union was North Korea. The United States and many of its allies fought to keep Communism out of South Korea in the Vietnam War. By the end of the war, nearby Vietnam faced a similar situation, with a Communist takeover of North Vietnam. The United States wanted to prevent South Vietnam from becoming Communist, and first tried to help the country establish a democracy. By the early 1960s, though, fighting broke out and the United States entered the century's fourth war. The Vietnam War remains the longest military conflict the United States has ever been involved in.

A REACTION TO THE COLD WAR

Since it was written in 1892, the Pledge of Allegiance has been meant to show loyalty to the United States and its flag. During the Cold War in 1954, Congress added the words "under God" to show the difference between America and Communist countries that were thought to be "Godless."

The Civil Rights Movement

At the time that the United States became independent, African Americans did not have the same rights as white Americans. After almost 200 years, although the laws of the country said they were equal, African Americans were not treated fairly. Blacks in the South were not allowed to vote, and were not allowed to go to the same schools as whites. Many public places, such as swimming pools and movie theaters, did not allow blacks. This practice of separating the races was known as segregation.

After World War II people around the country began speaking out against segregation and other types of inequality. They joined together as a movement in 1955, when a strong leader emerged. Dr. Martin Luther King Jr. attracted many people, black and white, to work for equality for African Americans. By 1963, under

Dr. King's leadership, over 1,000 demonstrations and protests were held across the South; President Kennedy sent a new civil rights bill to Congress; and in August over 200,000 people attended the March on Washington. The march was the largest political protest in U.S. history at that time. Congress passed Kennedy's bill the following year, six months after Kennedy was assassinated.

Like the laws passed 100 years earlier that freed slaves and gave them limited rights, the Civil Rights Act did not change the way people thought and behaved. Black churches were bombed, and many protesters were injured, jailed, or murdered. Martin Luther King continued to lead peaceful protests until 1968, when he was assassinated, days before Congress passed another civil rights bill.

The End of the Cold War

During the 1970s and 1980s, the Cold War continued as the two world superpowers—the Soviet Union and United States—remained enemies. During that time, many of the countries that made up the Soviet Union wanted to be democratic, and fought against the Soviet Union for their freedom. The United States supported many of those countries with money and weapons. In 1985, the Soviet Union's new leader, Mikhail Gorbachev, realized the need for a better relationship with America. He met with President Reagan, and the two superpowers signed the INF Treaty, promising to destroy many nuclear weapons.

By 1990, the Soviet Union was falling apart. Many of its republics (countries that had been taken over by the Soviet Union and made Communist) declared their independence. Months before the government voted to end the Soviet Union, Gorbachev met with President George H. W. Bush and the two signed a second treaty, agreeing to limit their numbers of nuclear weapons even more.

In 1991, the Soviet Union was divided into four independent countries: Belarus, Kazakhstan, Russia, and Ukraine. Russia was no longer a superpower; it had an improved relationship with the United States, and the two countries agreed to reduce their numbers of weapons. The Cold War was over.

Fifth War and Terrorist Attack

In 1990, Iraq invaded neighboring Kuwait. The United Nations placed sanctions, or restrictions, against Iraq to try to get them to leave Kuwait. This was unsuccessful, and in January of 1991, 12 countries, including the United States, fought the Iraqi army in the Persian Gulf War for one month, when the Iraqis were defeated.

Ten years later, a group of terrorists, most from Saudi Arabia, took over four passenger planes on the morning of September 11, 2001. They crashed two of the planes into the World Trade Towers in New York City, causing the towers to fall. Another plane flew into the Pentagon, and the fourth crashed in a field in Pennsylvania. The terrorists' leader, Osama bin Laden, made a statement saying that the attacks were carried out in part because of the United States' treatment of Muslims in Palestine, Somalia, and other areas.

Practice Questions

1. The president during World War I was _____.

2. One of the wars fought by the United States in the 1900s was _____.

3. Which president helped America to recover from the Great Depression and led us through World War II? _____

   _____

4. During World War II, the United States fought _____.

5. President Eisenhower was a general in what war? _____

6. When we say the Pledge of Allegiance, we show loyalty to _____.

7. The United States' main concern during the Cold War was _____.

8. The movement that worked to end racial discrimination was the_____

   _____

9. Who was Dr. Martin Luther King? _____.

10. What happened on September 1, 2001? _____

Answers and Explanations

1. Woodrow Wilson

   Explanation: Woodrow Wilson served as president from 1913-1921

2. Any one of the following is correct: World War I, World War II, Korean War, Vietnam War, Persian Gulf War.

3. Franklin Roosevelt

   Explanation: Franklin Roosevelt served as president from 1933-1945, leading the country out of the Great Depression and through World War II.

4. Japan, Germany, and Italy

   Explanation: Japan's bombing of Pearl Harbor brought the United States into World War II, but Japan had formed an alliance with Germany and Italy known as the Axis Alliance. Therefore, America fought against not just Japan but its allies as well.

5. World War II

   Explanation: Eisenhower was commanding general of our military, leading them to victory in World War II. He served as president for two terms, from 1953-1961.

6. The United States or the flag

   Explanation: The Pledge of Allegiance is a show of loyalty to our country and our flag.

7. Communism

   Explanation: After World War II, the Soviet Union began taking over countries and making them Communist. The United States wanted to stop the spread of Communism. The conflict between the Soviet Union and the United States was called the Cold War because it was never fought directly.

8. civil rights movement

   Explanation: In the 1950s and 1960s, African Americans began to protest the way they were being treated. They became organized under the leadership of Dr. Martin Luther King Jr., and worked to gain their civil rights.

9. Dr. Martin Luther King was an African American who led the civil rights movement in the 1950s and 1960s, fighting for civil rights and equality for all Americans.

   Explanation: Under Dr. King's leadership, protestors joined together to form the civil rights movement, which worked to end unfair treatment of African Americans. King led the movement from 1955 until he was assassinated in 1968.

10. the United States was attacked by terrorists

   Explanation: Terrorists took over four passenger planes, crashing two into the World Trade Towers in New York and one into the Pentagon in Washington. The fourth plane crashed in a field in Pennsylvania.

FEDERAL AND STATE POWERS

In this section, you learn the information you need to know about the U.S. government in order to pass the civics test given during your USCIS interview.

The Constitution explains how the organization of the government, including the election process of leaders and the kinds of powers they can and cannot have. Most states use a system for their government that is similar to the one used by the federal government.

Important Terms and Names

checks and balances   judicial branch

separation of powers   Supreme Court

executive branch   cabinet

legislative branch   Electoral College

Senate   governor

House of Representatives

Three Branches of Government: "Separation of Powers"

To make sure that the United States would not be ruled by one person, or even one group, the writers of the Constitution created a government in which power was separated into three branches. This separation of power is supposed to provide checks and balances. Each branch can "check" on the others to make sure that they are working the way they are supposed to, and that no one branch has all the power—it is "balanced" among the three.

The Executive Branch

The president heads the first, or executive, branch of the government, and it includes the vice president and the members of the president's cabinet (his or her advisors). It is the president's job to execute, or carry out, federal laws and recommend new ones; command the armed forces; direct national defense and foreign policy; deal with foreign governments; and perform ceremonial duties. The president can veto, or reject, bills passed by Congress so they do not become laws. The president is elected every four years in November, and is sworn in, or inaugurated, in January of the following year. Once inaugurated, the president and his or her family move to the White House in Washington, D.C. where they live for the length of his or her term.

HOW IS A PRESIDENT ELECTED?

When voters go to the polls on Election Day, they're not really voting for the president. Each state has a group of "electors" who pledge to vote for the candidate who gets the most votes from the people (known as the state's popular vote). The number of electors equals the number of that state's members of Congress (two senators plus the number of representatives, which is based on population size), so some states have more electoral votes than others do. About a month after the election, the Electoral College meets to choose the president officially. Because the electors almost always vote for the candidate who won the popular vote, it is easy to figure out who will win the Electoral College votes for each state by seeing who won the popular vote in that state.

The Legislative Branch

Congress heads the second branch, or legislative branch, of the government. Two bodies make up Congress, the House of Representatives, which has 435 members, and the Senate, which has two senators from every state (100 total). The number of representatives for each state is based on population, which is why Vermont has one representative and California has over 50. States vote for their own representatives and senators. Representatives serve two-year terms, and senators serve six-year terms; there is no limit to the number of terms they may serve.

Congress's job is to make laws. Laws begin as bills, which are introduced in the House and the Senate. If a bill gets a majority of votes in both the House and Senate, it becomes a law. Congress also has the power to declare war, write spending bills (House), impeach officials (Senate), and approve presidential nominations and treaties (Senate).

The Judicial Branch

The Supreme Court heads the third, or judicial, branch, and it includes all of the courts in the United States court system. The Supreme Court is made up of nine justices who are appointed by a president, and who have no term limit. The judicial branch's powers include interpreting the Constitution, reviewing laws, and deciding cases involving states' rights. The Supreme Court is the highest court in the land, and its decisions cannot be overturned by any other court.

Branches of State and Local Governments

In addition to the federal government, states, cities, and towns have their own governments. Most states use a three-branch system that is similar to the structure of the federal government. Instead of a president, states are led by a governor, who is the head of the executive branch. Cities and towns elect a mayor to lead them.

States also have a legislative branch made up of two bodies (except for Nebraska, which has one) that go by different names. Some states call them the Senate and House of Representatives, and others have a General Assembly instead of a House of Representatives. State legislative bodies, like federal ones, have the power to make laws. In cities and towns, citizens elect people to serve on city councils. These legislative bodies also make laws.

The United States court system is made up of many courts that have different levels of authority. State courts range from the Supreme Court, which is the highest in the state, to county and city courts, which hear local cases. Higher courts can review many of the decisions made by lower courts.

Practice Questions

1. No one branch of government can become too powerful because of

_____.

2. Who leads the executive branch? _____

3. Who can sign bills into law or veto bills? _____

4. Name two positions in the president's cabinet (his advisors).

_____

5. Some states have more representative than others because

_____

6. How long are the terms for representatives and senators? _____

7. Senators are elected to represent _____

8. Which branch of government makes laws? _____

_____

9. The highest court in the land, which heads the judicial branch, is _____,
   made up of _____ justices.

10. The judicial branch does what? _____

Answers and Explanations

1. separation of powers or checks and balances

   Explanation: The writers of the Constitution did not want all of the power to go to one person or one group. They believed the three branches would prevent that from happening.

2. the president

   Explanation: The president has the power to sign bills into law and to veto them. This is part of the checks and balances system that prevents one part of our government from having too much power. The president can "check" the Congress' power by vetoing bills.

3. the president

   Explanation: The president has the power to sign bills into law and to veto them. This is part of the checks and balances system that prevents one part of our government from having too much power. The president can "check" the Congress' power by vetoing bills.

4. Answers will vary, but must include two from the following list: Secretary of Agriculture, Secretary of Commerce, Secretary of Defense, Secretary of Education, Secretary of Energy, Secretary of Health and Human Services, Secretary of Homeland Security, Secretary of Housing and Urban Development, Secretary of the Interior, Secretary of Labor, Secretary of State, Secretary of Transportation, Secretary of the Treasury, Secretary of Veterans Affairs, Attorney General, Vice President.

   Explanation: There are currently 16 cabinet-level positions, all in the executive branch. The cabinet members serve as advisors to the president.

5. because of the state's population

   Explanation: The number of representatives each state has is based on how many people live in that state. California is the most populous state, and has the most representatives (53). States with considerably fewer people, such as Alaska, Montana, and Vermont, have one representative.

6. two years for representatives and six years for senators

   Explanation: We elect representatives every two years and senators every six years. They can serve as many terms as they are elected for.

7. everyone in their state

   Explanation: States vote for their senators, who represent everyone in that state.

8. Legislative (Congress, House of Representatives and Senate)

   Explanation: The Congress makes federal laws by first writing bills. When the president signs a bill, it becomes law.

9. the Supreme Court; nine

   Explanation: The highest court in the United States, the one with the most power, is the Supreme Court. The number of justices has varied from seven to 10, but since 1869 there have been nine.

10. reviews and explains laws, resolves disagreements or disputes, and decides if laws go against the Constitution

    Explanation: The judicial branch is made up of our courts.

CITIZENS' RIGHTS AND THE CONSTITUTION

As soon as the Constitution was written, it was changed. These changes, called amendments, have been made throughout the history of the United States.

Important Terms and Names

supreme law of the land   freedom of religion

amendment   freedom of the press

term limit   right to bear arms

Bill of Rights   voter

freedom of speech   Pledge of Allegiance

The U.S. Constitution and Important Principles

The United States Constitution explains the U.S. form of government and laws. It was written in 1787 by leaders from each state. Because these leaders had once been ruled by a country with one all-powerful leader (the king) they knew the kinds of problems created by that form of government, and they wanted something different.

There are three parts to the Constitution:

1. Preamble—The preamble is the introduction that explains the Constitution and the government it describes.

2. Articles—The seven articles explain the government's structure.

3. Amendments—The amendments are the changes to the original seven articles.

The Constitution has four basic principles:

1. There are three branches of government (executive, legislative, judicial) that separate and balance powers.

2. The Constitution is the supreme law of the land, meaning that no other laws come above it.

3. All people and all states are equal before the law, and each state must be democratic and respect the law of other states.

4. The Constitution can be changed according to the methods outlined in it.

The fourth principle says it is possible to change, or amend, the Constitution. In order to suggest a change, or amendment, the House and Senate must have a two-thirds vote, or two-thirds of the states must call for a national convention to consider the amendment. To add an amendment to the Constitution, three-fourths of the states must vote for it. There are currently 27 amendments.

The Constitution also explains how the office of president works. To be elected to that office, a person must be a natural-born citizen of the United States, be at least 35 years old, and have lived in the United States for at least 14 years. If the president dies before completing his or her term, the vice president becomes president. If the president and vice president die, the leader of the House of Representatives, also called the Speaker of the House, becomes president. An amendment added in 1951 puts a term limit on the office; presidents can serve a maximum of two terms.

Bill of Rights

After the Constitution was written, some states would not sign it unless it protected citizens' freedoms and limited the power of the federal government. Ten amendments were written to provide those protections. When they were added to the Constitution, all the states signed it. The 10 amendments are called the Bill of Rights.

Bill of Rights

1. Grants freedom of worship, speech, the press, right of peaceful assembly, right to petition the government

2. Grants right of citizens to bear arms (weapons)

3. Says troops may not be quartered in private homes without the owner's consent

4. Guards against unreasonable searches, arrests, seizures of property

5–8. Provide protection for people who are accused of crimes

9. Says that people have more rights than just those mentioned in the Constitution

10. Grants that powers not assigned to the federal government belong to the states or the people

POLITICAL PARTIES

In the United States, many organizations can try to gain power by putting candidates in elections. These organizations are called political parties. There are two major parties that hold most elected offices and have the most registered voters as members: the Democratic Party, which was founded about 1828, and the Republican Party, founded in 1854. Other parties that are currently active include the Libertarian Party, the Green Party, and the Constitution Party.

Voting in Elections

The right to vote in an American election has its own history. For hundreds of years, people were kept from voting for various reasons, including their gender, race, ability to read, land ownership, and income. Through a number of amendments to the Constitution, those reasons are now illegal. However, in some states people who are serving time in prison, those who once committed a serious crime, and/or those with certain mental incapacities cannot vote.

To vote, you must be a United States citizen who is at least 18 years old. Before an election, you must register to vote by contacting your local election office, which is listed in the phonebook. Election offices are often called the county clerk's office or municipal board of elections. If you cannot find a listing, contact your state board of elections or check with your local library. A few weeks after registering, you should receive a notice in the mail that confirms your registration and tells you where to go to vote.

Pledge of Allegiance

The oath of allegiance to the country and its flag was written in 1892, and was changed twice before taking the form it has today. The word "flag" was changed to "flag of the United States of America" in 1924, and in 1954 the words "under God" were added. The Pledge, which is spoken with the right hand over the heart, is often recited at public events, and is currently required in the classrooms of 35 states.

THE PLEDGE OF ALLEGIANCE

I pledge allegiance to the Flag of the United States of America
and to the Republic for which it stands, one nation, under God,
indivisible, with liberty and justice for all.

Practice Questions

1. What is the Bill of Rights? _____

   _____

   _____

2. If the president dies, the _____
   becomes president.

3. To be eligible to vote, you must be at least _____ years old.

4. A president can serve for up to _____ terms.

5. Can all citizens of legal age vote? _____

6. The Constitution can be changed by adding a(n) _____

   _____.

7. What are three rights or freedoms guaranteed by the Bill of Rights?

   _____

   _____

   _____

8. The words _____
   were added to the Pledge of Allegiance in 1954.

9. Before you can vote, you need to _____.

10. A person must be at least _____ years of age to run for president.

Answers and Explanations

1. The first 10 amendments to the Constitution make up the Bill of Rights.

   Explanation: These amendments limit the power of the federal government and protect people's freedoms.

2. The vice president becomes president if the president dies.

   Explanation: The writers of the Constitution wanted to make sure that, if the president died, no individual or group would try to take over the government. They explained exactly what would happen if the president, and even the vice president died, so that there would be a smooth transition from one leader to another.

3. You must be at least 18 years of age to vote.

4. A president can serve two four-year terms.

   Explanation: After Franklin Roosevelt was elected to a fourth term, many Americans wanted term limits. They worried that a president could become too powerful if he or she served more than eight years, thus upsetting the balance of power and system of checks and balances.

5. No, not all citizens are allowed to vote.

   Explanation: Every citizen over the age of 18 is allowed to vote in most states. However, some states do not allow prisoners, former prisoners who committed serious crimes, and/or people with certain mental incapacities the right to vote.

6. The Constitution can be changed by adding an amendment.

7. The Bill of Rights guarantees freedom of worship, freedom of speech, and freedom of the press; the right of peaceful assembly, the right to petition the government, and the right to bear arms.

   Explanation: After the Constitution was written, some states would not sign it unless it provided protections for citizens against violations of their rights by the government, and limited the power of the federal government. Therefore, 10 amendments were added to secure these rights.

8. The words "under God" were added to the Pledge of Allegiance in 1954.

9. In order to vote, you must register.

10. Thirty-five is the minimum age one must be to run for president.

STEP 4 REVIEW

The following questions are similar to those you will have to answer during your USCIS interview.

Civics Practice Questions

Write the correct answer or circle the letter next to the correct answer choice.

1. The United States Supreme Court has _____ justices.

2. Why did the Pilgrims come to America? _____

_____

_____

3. The last states to be added to the United States were _____

and _____.

4. Why wasn't the Jamestown colony successful?

a. It did not have the help of Native Americans.

b. Its tobacco crop failed.

c. The settlers moved south after the first winter.

d. It didn't have a good leader.

5. Who becomes the country's leader if the president is unable to complete his or her term? _____

_____

_____

6. When saying the Pledge of Allegiance, put your _____ hand over your heart.

7. What did most Southern states do when Abraham Lincoln was elected president?

_____

_____

_____

8. Segregation kept African Americans from being allowed to

a. register to vote.

b. hold government jobs.

c. attend schools with white children.

d. travel freely between states.

9. What was the Underground Railroad? _____

_____

_____

10. Who is the leader of the executive branch in local government? _____

_____

_____

11. The national anthem is _____

_____

_____ .

12. One of America's allies during World War II was

a. Japan.

b. England.

c. Italy.

d. Germany.

13. What happened at Pearl Harbor? _____

_____

_____

14. What was the civil rights movement? _____

_____

_____

15. When a state was added, what happened to the stars and stripes on the flag?

_____

_____

_____

16. In which document did Thomas Jefferson write, "All men are created equal"?

    a. the Constitution

    b. the Bill of Rights

    c. the Declaration of Independence

    d. the Mayflower Compact

17. Can the Constitution be changed? _____

18. Which countries were involved in the Cold War? _____

_____

19. The two sides fighting the Civil War were called _____

and _____.

20. Who elects the president?

    a. the people

    b. the Senate

    c. the House of Representatives

    d. the Electoral College

ANSWERS AND EXPLANATIONS

1. Nine justices sit on the U.S. Supreme Court.

2. The Pilgrims came so they could freely practice their religion. The king of England did not allow the Pilgrims to practice their religion in that country.

3. Alaska and Hawaii were the last states to be added.

4. (a) The Jamestown colony was not successful because it did not have the help of Native Americans. The members of the Jamestown colony, unlike the Pilgrims in the colony at Plymouth, did not have a good relationship with the Native Americans living nearby.

5. In the event that the president is unable to finish his or her term, the vice president is next in line to become president.

6. When saying the Pledge of Allegiance, one should place the right hand over the heart.

7. They left the Union and formed the Confederate States of America.

   Explanation: Southern states held slaves, and they knew Abraham Lincoln was against slavery. They did not want to be ruled by someone who would try to take away their slaves, so they joined together and elected their own president.

8. (c) Segregation kept African Americans from being allowed to attend schools with white children.

   Explanation: Segregation meant that blacks and whites used separate facilities, including schools, public restrooms, and recreational facilities like pools.

9. The Underground Railroad was a system that helped Southern slaves escape to freedom in the North. However, it was neither underground nor a railroad. It was a number of different routes formed by Northerners, including freed slaves. Many people helped the slaves on these routes, hiding them and traveling with them until they reached a free state.

10. A mayor is the leader of local government. Citizens of towns and cities elect a mayor to lead their executive branch of government.

11. "The Star-Spangled Banner" is the national anthem.

12. (b) England and the United States were allies during World War II.

    Explanation: Japan, Italy, and Germany were enemies of the United States.

13. The Japanese bombed the U.S. Navy base there in 1941, provoking America to enter World War II. Until the bombing, the United States did not want to get involved with the war. After the attack, it declared war on Japan, and the next day Japan's allies, Germany and Italy, declared war on the United States.

14. The civil rights movement was a struggle for equality for African Americans. In 1955, Dr. Martin Luther King Jr. and his followers began protesting the unfair treatment of African Americans. During the 1960s, protests continued, including the March on Washington in 1963. Congress passed two civil rights bills, but problems continued.

15. A star was added, but the number of stripes remained the same. There are 50 stars on the flag, one for every state. The 13 stripes never changed—they represent the original 13 colonies.

16. (c) The Declaration of Independence, authored by Jefferson, declared that all people were equal and that the colonists deserved independence from England.

17. Yes, the Constitution can be changed by adding amendments. To suggest an amendment, the House and Senate must have a two-thirds vote, or two-thirds of the states must call for a national convention to consider the amendment. To add an amendment to the Constitution, three-fourths of the states must vote for it.

18. The Soviet Union and United States were the two superpowers that were involved in the Cold War.

    Explanation: Although it was called a war, there was no actual fighting during the Cold War. The superpowers made so many nuclear weapons that they knew they would destroy each other if they ever used them. This fear of destruction kept both countries from wanting to fight directly.

19. Confederate and Union, or South and North

20. (d) The Electoral College, made up of "electors" from each state, chooses the president. The electors' votes are based on the votes of citizens in the states they represent.

NOTES

_____

_____

_____

_____

_____

_____

_____

_____

_____

_____

_____

_____

_____

_____

_____

_____

_____

_____

_____

_____

_____

_____

Step 5: **Take the English Communication Practice Test**

Remember that during your interview your ability to read, write, and speak English is tested. The following exercises help you practice these skills. If you encounter any unfamiliar words, write them down in the Notes section at the end of this chapter, or on a separate piece of paper, and look up their definitions using a dictionary or the Glossary at the end of this book.

PRACTICE READING

The reading test will be no longer than three sentences. You must be able to read at least one of the sentences correctly. All of the sentences below use only the words found on the Reading Vocabulary list in Step 3. Practice reading these sentences out loud:

1. There are 100 senators in Congress.

2. I want to be an American citizen.

3. The first president was George Washington.

4. Congress meets in the Capitol building.

5. The American flag is red, white, and blue.

6. America has 50 states.

7. Abraham Lincoln was a U.S. president.

8. Citizens can vote.

9. When is Thanksgiving?

10. What is the Bill of Rights?

PRACTICE WRITING

For the writing test, you will be read no more than three sentences and have to write them. The sentences below use only the works found on the Writing Vocabulary list in Step 3. You can practice by copying them and by having someone read them to you as you write them on a separate piece of paper.

1. Lincoln was president during the Civil War.

2. Delaware was the first state.

3. Canada is north of the United States.

4. Washington was Father of Our Country.

5. Freedom of speech is a right of citizens.

6. Presidents' Day is in February.

7. Washington, D.C., is the capital of the United States.

8. California is south of Alaska.

9. Citizens pay taxes.

10. Independence Day is in July.

11. The largest state is Alaska.

12. Labor Day is in September.

13. Mexico is south of the United States.

14. Most people want to be free.

15. Columbus Day is in October.

PRACTICE SPEAKING

During your interview, your interviewer will pay attention to how well you speak English. He or she will ask you questions about yourself. Expect to be asked some of the questions on the following list. Practice answering them out loud.

1. Have you ever used other names?

2. Are you at least 18 years old?

3. What is your current marital status?

4. What is your mailing address?

5. Where have you lived during the last five years?

6. How many days did you spend outside the United States in the last five years?

7. If you are married, what is your spouse's name?

8. How many sons and daughters do you have?

9. Have you ever voted in a United States election?

10. Do you owe any overdue federal, state, or local taxes?

11. Have you ever been charged with committing a crime?

12. Have you ever served in the United States military?

13. When required by law, are you willing to bear arms for the United States?

14. Is your spouse a citizen of the United States?

15. Do you understand the Oath of Allegiance to the United States?

_____

NOTES

_____

_____

_____

_____

_____

_____

_____

_____

_____

_____

_____

_____

_____

_____

_____

_____

_____

_____

_____

_____

Step 6: **Take the Civics Practice Test**

You will be asked 10 of the following 100 questions, and must answer at least six of them correctly. Some of these questions can be answered in different ways, but the responses in the Answers and Explanation section are the ones you should know.

Note: If you are 65 or older and have been a legal permanent resident for at least 20 years, you should study only the first 20 questions. You will not be asked any of the other questions on this list.

SHORT-ANSWER QUESTIONS

1. Name one of the rights or freedoms guaranteed in the First Amendment.

   _____

   _____

2. What kind of economic system does the United States have? _____

   _____

   _____

3. Name one branch or part of our government. _____

   _____

   _____

4. Name the two parts of the Congress. _____

_____

_____

5. Name one of your state's U.S. senators who is serving right now. _____

_____

_____

6. In what month is the presidential election? _____

_____

_____

7. Who is the current president? _____

_____

_____

8. What is the capital of your state?_____

_____

_____

9. What are the two major political parties in the United States?_____

_____

_____

10. Name a responsibility of United States citizen. _____

_____

_____

11. To vote for president, how old do citizens have to be? _____

_____

_____

12. When is the last day you can send in federal income tax forms? _____

_____

_____

13. Who was the first president? _____

_____

_____

14. What was one thing that President Lincoln did?_____

_____

_____

15. What was one of the wars fought by the United States in the 1900s? ___

_____

_____

16. What did Martin Luther King Jr. do?_____

_____

_____

17. What is the capital of the United States?_____

_____

_____

18. Where is the Statue of Liberty? _____

_____

_____

19. Why does the flag have 50 stars? _____

_____

_____

20. What is the date of Independence Day?_____

_____

_____

21. What is the supreme law of the land?_____

_____

_____

22. The Constitution does what?_____

_____

_____

23. What are the first three words of the Constitution? These are the words that present the idea of self-government.

_____

_____

_____

24. An amendment to the Constitution is what? _____

_____

_____

25. The first 10 amendments to the Constitution are called what?_____

_____

_____

26. How many amendments have been made to the Constitution? _____

_____

_____

27. The Declaration of Independence did what? _____

_____

_____

28. Name two rights from the Declaration of Independence. _____

_____

_____ _____

29. Freedom of religion is what? _____

_____

_____

30. The "rule of law" is what? _____

_____

_____

31. One branch of government is stopped from becoming too powerful
    by what? _____

_____

_____

32. Who is the head of the executive branch of government? _____

_____

_____

33. Who makes federal laws? _____

_____

_____

34. How many senators are there? _____

_____

_____

35. How long is a senator's term? _____

_____

_____

36. How many voting members are currently serving in the House of Representatives? _____

_____

_____

37. How long is a term for a member of the House of representatives? _____

_____

_____

38. Name your U.S. Representative. _____

_____

_____

39. A U.S. senator represents who?_____

_____

_____

40. Some states have more representatives than other states. Why? _____

_____

_____

41. How long is a presidential term?_____

_____

_____

42. Who is the current vice president? _____

_____

_____

43. Who becomes president if the president can no longer serve? _____

_____

_____

44. Who becomes president if the president and vice-president can no
longer serve?

_____

_____

45. Who is the commander in chief of the military?_____

_____

_____

46. Bills are signed into laws by who?_____

_____

_____

47. Who can veto bills?_____

_____

_____

48. What does the president's cabinet do?_____

_____

_____

49. Name two positions in the president's cabinet. _____

_____

_____

50. What does the judicial branch do? _____

_____

_____

51. The highest court in the United States is what? _____

_____

_____

52. How many Supreme Court justices are there?_____

_____

_____

53. Who is the current chief justice of the United States? _____

_____

_____

54. Name one power of the federal government. _____

_____

_____

55. Name one power of the states. _____

_____

_____

56. Who is the current governor of your state?_____

_____

_____

57. What is the current president's political party? _____

_____

_____

58. Who is the current Speaker of the House of Representatives? _____

_____

_____

59. Describe one of the four amendments to the Constitution about who can vote._____

_____

_____

60. Name one of the rights of United States citizens. _____

_____

_____

61. Name two rights of everyone living in the United States. _____

_____

_____

62. When we say the Pledge of Allegiance, what do we show loyalty to? ___

_____

_____

63. When you become a United States citizen, what is one of the promises you make?_____

_____

_____

64. What are two ways American citizens can participate in their democracy?

_____

_____

65. All men register for the Selective Service when? _____

_____

_____

66. What is one reason colonists came to America? _____

_____

_____

67. Who lived in America before the Europeans arrived?_____

_____

_____

68. What group of people was taken to America and sold as slaves?_____

_____

_____

69. The colonists fought the British for what reason?_____

_____

_____

70. Who wrote the Declaration of Independence?_____

_____

_____

71. When was the Declaration of Independence adopted?_____

_____

_____

72. Name three of the original 13 colonies. _____

_____

_____

73. What happened at the Constitutional Convention? _____

_____

_____

74. When was the Constitution written? _____

_____

_____

75. Name one of the writers of the Federalist Papers (these papers supported the passage of the U.S. Constitution). _____

_____

_____

76. Name one thing Benjamin Franklin is famous for. _____

_____

_____

77. Who is the "Father of Our Country"? _____

_____

_____

78. The United States bought a territory from France in 1803. What was it?

_____

_____

79. What was one of the wars fought by the United States in the 1800s? ___

_____

_____

80. What was the U.S. war fought between the North and the South? _____

_____

_____

81. Name one of the problems that caused the Civil War. _____

_____

_____

82. What did the Emancipation Proclamation do? _____

_____

_____

83. Name one thing Susan B. Anthony is known for. _____

_____

_____

84. The president during World War I was who? _____

_____

_____

85. Name the president who served during the Great Depression and
World War II. _____

_____

_____

86. Who did the United States fight in World War II? _____

_____

_____

87. President Eisenhower was once a general in what war? _____

_____

_____

88. What was the main concern of the United States during the Cold War,?

_____

_____

89. Name the movement that tried to end racial discrimination. _____

_____

_____

90. On September 11, 2001, what event happened in the United States?

_____

_____

91. There are many American Indian tribes in the United States. Name one.

_____

_____

92. What is one of the two longest rivers in the United States?_____

_____

_____

93. Name the ocean on the West Coast of the United States. _____

_____

_____

94. Name the ocean on the East Coast of the United States. _____

_____

_____

95. What is one U.S. territory? _____

_____

_____

96. What is one state that borders Canada? _____

_____

_____

97. What is one state that borders Mexico? _____

_____

_____

98. Why does the flag have 13 stripes? _____

_____

_____

99. Name the national anthem. _____

_____

_____

100. What are two national U.S. holidays? _____

_____

_____

ANSWERS AND EXPLANATIONS

1. Any one of the following is correct: freedom of speech, freedom of religion, freedom of assembly, freedom of the press, or freedom to petition the government.

   Explanation: The First Amendment to the Constitution gives all Americans five specific rights or freedoms.

2. a capitalist, or market, economy

   Explanation: In a capitalist or market economy, individuals have money and make decisions about how it is spent and invested.

3. Any one of the following is correct: Congress, legislative, president, executive, the courts, judicial.

   Explanation: There are three parts or branches in the government, all with equal power. They are known as the legislative branch or the Congress, the executive branch headed by the president, and the judicial branch which is made up of the courts.

4. the Senate and the House of Representatives

   Explanation: Federal laws are made by the legislative branch, which is also known as the Congress, and as its two parts, the House of Representatives and Senate.

5. Answers will vary. Residents of Washington, D.C.; Puerto Rico; American Samoa; Guam; the United States Virgin Islands; and the Commonwealth of the Northern Mariana Islands should know that they have no representation in the Senate.

   Explanation: All 50 states have senators in Congress. The five territories and Washington, D.C. have no senators.

6. November

   Explanation: The presidential election is held every four years on the Tuesday between November 2 and November 8.

7. Barack Obama, or Obama

   Explanation: Barack Obama is the current president, elected in November of 2008 and inaugurated on January 20, 2009.

8. Answers will vary. Applicants who live in the District of Columbia must answer that D.C. does not have a capital because it is not a state. Applicants who live in U.S. territories must name the capital of the territory.

   Explanation: Each state's government is based in the state capital.

9. Democratic and Republican

   Explanation: Although there are many political parties in the Unites States, there are only two major ones. Since 1853, every president has been either a Democrat or a Republican.

10. either serving on a jury or voting in a federal election

    Explanation: The two responsibilities of American citizens only are to serve on a jury and to vote in a federal election.

11. 18 or older

    Explanation: Since 1971, Americans have had to be at least 18 years old to vote for president.

12. April 15th

    Explanation: You can send in federal income tax forms as soon as you have all of the information you need to fill them out (usually by the end of January), but they must be mailed by April 15th at the latest.

13. George Washington

    Explanation: Washington was chosen unanimously by the delegates of the Constitutional Convention to be our first president in 1787.

14. Any one of the following is correct: freed the slaves (Emancipation Proclamation), saved the Union (kept the country from being divided), was our leader during the Civil War.

    Explanation: Abraham Lincoln was one of the United States' greatest presidents. He served during the Civil War, and is given credit for keeping the country together when Southern states tried to form their own union (called the Confederacy). At the end of the war, he signed the Emancipation Proclamation, which freed the slaves.

15. Any one of the following is correct: World War I, World War II, Korean War, Vietnam War, Persian Gulf War (or Gulf War).

    Explanation: The American military fought in five wars during the 1900s, none of which took place on American soil.

16. Either answer is correct: wanted or fought for civil rights, worked for equality for all Americans, no matter what race they were.

    Explanation: During the civil rights movement of the 1950s and 1960s, Dr. King became a leader who helped organize African Americans and their white supporters to speak out against injustice and demand equality.

17. Washington, D.C.

    Explanation: Washington, D.C. has been the capital of the United States since 1791.

18. Any one of the following is correct: New York (Harbor), Liberty Island, New Jersey, near New York City, on the Hudson (River).

    Explanation: The Statue of Liberty was a gift to the United States from France. When it arrived in 1885 it was placed on a 12-acre island in New York Harbor.

19. Any one of the following is correct: because there is one star for each state, because each star represents a state, because there are 50 states

    Explanation: The flag began with 13 stars. Between 1794 and 1960, 37 stars were added, one for each state that was added to the Union.

20. July 4

    Explanation: July 4th is the day the Continental Congress signed the Declaration of Independence.

21. the Constitution

    Explanation: The Constitution is called the supreme law of the Land because no other laws, including those of state governments, can take its place.

22. defines and sets up the government; protects the basic rights of Americans

    Explanation: The Constitution explains the branches of government; term limits for Congress, the president and vice-president, and Supreme Court justices; the powers of each branch and their limits; who can be president; and the protections given to every American.

23. "We the People"

    Explanation: These words establish the idea of self-government. It is a government made by the people for the people.

24. a change or addition to the Constitution

    Explanation: The Constitution explains how it can be changed or added to. An amendment begins by Congress writing a bill that is passed by a two thirds majority in both the House and Senate. Then it must be passed, or "ratified" by three quarters of the states.

25. the Bill of Rights

    Explanation: These amendments were added to the Constitution to make sure all Americans were protected by certain rights, including the right to a speedy trial if accused of a crime, and the right to own weapons.

26. 27

    Explanation: From 1791 to 1992, there have been 27 changes or additions to the Constitution, including the 19th, which gave women the right to vote, and the 13th, which abolished slavery.

27. Either one of the following is correct: announced or declared our independence (from Great Britain), said that the United States is free (from Great Britain).

    Explanation: Thomas Jefferson wrote in the Declaration of Independence that the 13 colonies of the United States were no longer going to be ruled by Great Britain's king.

28. Any two of the following is correct: the right to life, liberty, and/or the pursuit of happiness.

    Explanation: Thomas Jefferson famously wrote that "All men are created equal," and were given by their Creator three rights (life, liberty, and the pursuit of happiness).

29. the right to be able to practice any religion or practice no religion

    Explanation: Many of the Europeans who came to America left their countries because they could not practice their religion the way they wanted to. It was very important to them that they, and everyone else, be allowed to practice any religion or even no religion without fear.

30. everyone, including leaders and our government, has to follow the law; no one is above the law

    Explanation: Thomas Paine wrote in 1776 that in some countries the king is law, but in free countries, the law is king. The rule of law means that everyone is equal under the law.

31. checks and balances or separation of powers

    Explanation: The three branches of government (judicial, executive, and legislative) have equal power, and perform different duties. They make sure one branch doesn't claim more power than it should or take on the duties of another branch.

32. the president

    Explanation: The executive branch includes the president, vice-president, cabinet, federal agencies, and the military. It is led by the President.

33. the congress, legislature, or House (of Representatives) and Senate

    Explanation: The Congress makes federal laws by first writing bills. When the president signs a bill, it becomes law.

34. 100

    Explanation: Every state elects two senators; because there are 50 states we have 100 senators.

35. six years

    Explanation: When we elect a senator he or she serves a six-year term.

36. there are 435 voting members of the House of Representatives

    Explanation: The House of Representative is supposed to represent the people rather than the states, so each member represents part of the population of a state. In 1929, the total number of representatives was set at 435.

37. two years

    Explanation: When we elect a representative, he or she serves a two year term.

38. Answers will vary. Residents of Washington, D.C., Puerto Rico; American Samoa; Guam; the United States Virgin Islands; and the Commonwealth of the Northern Mariana Islands should know that they are represented in the House of Representatives only, by a nonvoting delegate.

    Explanation: In states that have one representative, all of the people of the state are represented by that person. U.S. Territories and Washington, D.C. have one representative each, but they are not allowed to vote. All other states have one or more representatives who represent the people of part of their state.

39. all of the people of his or her state

    Explanation: States vote for their senators, who represent everyone in that state.

40. Any of the following is correct: because they have more people, because some states have more people, because of the state's population.

    Explanation: The number of representatives each state has is based on how many people live in that state. California is the most populous state, and has the most representatives (53). States with considerably fewer people, such as Alaska, Montana, and Vermont, have one representative.

41. four years

    Explanation: Presidents are elected to serve one four-year term (although they can serve up to two terms if they are elected twice).

42. Joseph or Joe Biden, or Biden

    Explanation: Joe Biden is our current vice-president, elected in November of 2008 and sworn in on January 20, 2009.

43. the vice-president

    Explanation: The Constitution explains the presidential line of succession, naming the vice-president as next in line if the president can no longer serve.

44. the Speaker of the House

    Explanation: The Constitution explains the presidential line of succession, naming the Speaker of the House as next in line if the president and vice-president can no longer serve.

45. the president

    Explanation: The Constitution gives the title Commander in Chief of the Army, Navy, and Militias to the President.

46. the president

    Explanation: The president has the power to sign bills into law. This is part of the checks and balances system that prevents one part of our government from having too much power.

47. the president

    Explanation: The president's veto power is explained in the Constitution. It is part of the system of checks and balances because it helps prevent the Congress from becoming too powerful. The president can check the Congress' power by vetoing bills.

48. advises the president

    Explanation: The president chooses his advisors, who together are called his cabinet. Congress must approve the cabinet members.

49. Answers will vary, but must include two from the following list: Secretary of Agriculture, Secretary of Commerce, Secretary of Defense, Secretary of Education, Secretary of Energy, Secretary of Health and Human Services, Secretary of Homeland Security, Secretary of Housing and Urban Development, Secretary of the Interior, Secretary of Labor, Secretary of State, Secretary of Transportation, Secretary of the Treasury, Secretary of Veterans Affairs, Attorney General, Vice President.

    Explanation: There are currently 16 cabinet-level positions, all in the executive branch. The cabinet members serve as advisors to the president.

50. reviews and explains laws, resolves disagreements or disputes, and decides if laws go against the Constitution

    Explanation: The judicial branch is made up of our courts.

51. the Supreme Court

    Explanation: The highest court in the United States, the one with the most power, is the Supreme Court.

52. nine

    Explanation: The number of justices has varied from seven to 10, but since 1869 there have been nine.

53. John Roberts

    Explanation: The current chief justice, John Roberts, was appointed by President George W. Bush in 2005.

54. Answers will vary, but must be one of the following: print money, declare war, create an army, or make treaties.

    Explanation: The Constitution explains the powers of the federal government, giving it the right to print money, declare war, create an army, and make treaties with other countries.

55. Answers will vary, but must be one of the following: to provide schooling and education, to provide protection (police), to provide safety (fire departments), to give driver's licenses, or to approve zoning and land use.

Explanation: The Constitution gives five powers to state governments. They are to provide schooling and education, to provide protection (police), to provide safety (fire departments), to give driver's licenses, and to approve zoning and land use.

56. Answers will vary. Applicants living in the District of Columbia must answer that D.C. does not have a governor.

Explanation: The head of every state government is called a governor. There are 50 governors in the United States.

57. Democratic

Explanation: President Barack Obama is a member of the Democratic Party.

58. Nancy Pelosi

Explanation: The current Speaker of the House of Representatives is Nancy Pelosi of California.

59. Any one of the following is correct: citizens 18 and older can vote; you don't have to pay (a poll tax) to vote; any citizen, male or female, can vote; a male citizen of any race can vote.

Explanation: The Constitution has been amended four times to explain who can vote. If you are a citizen of either gender or any race who is 18 or older, you can vote. There is no fee or tax charged for voting.

60. A correct answer is either voting in a federal election or running for a federal office.

Explanation: Two rights for American citizens only are to vote in a federal election and to run for federal office.

61. Answers will vary, but must be two of the following: freedom of expression, freedom of speech, freedom of assembly, freedom to petition the government, freedom of worship, the right to bear arms.

Explanation: The Bill of Rights gives everyone living in the United States, whether they are citizens or not, these six rights.

62. A correct answer is either the United States or the flag.

    Explanation: The Pledge of Allegiance is a show of loyalty to our country and our flag.

63. Answers will vary, but must be one of the following: give up loyalty to other countries, defend the Constitution and laws of the United States, obey the laws of the United States, serve in the U.S. military if needed, serve the nation if needed, be loyal to the United States.

    Explanation: During the Citizenship ceremony, new citizens make six promises which are to give up loyalty to other countries, defend the Constitution and laws of the United States, obey the laws of the United States, serve in the U.S. military if needed, serve the nation if needed, and to be loyal to the United States.

64. Answers will vary but must be two of the following: vote, join a political party, help with a campaign, join a civic group, join a community group, give an elected official your opinion on an issue, call senators and representatives, publicly support or oppose an issue or policy, run for office, and write to a newspaper.

    Explanation: There are 10 ways for Americans to participate in their democracy.

65. A correct answer is 18 or between 18 and 26.

    Explanation: All men between the ages of 18 and 26, whether citizens or noncitizens living permanently in the United States must, register for Selective Service.

66. Answers will vary but must be one of the following: freedom, political liberty, freedom to practice their religion, economic opportunity, or to escape persecution.

    Explanation: Immigrants have been coming to America since colonial times, because they believe it gives them the chance to have better lives than the ones they led in their native countries. That could mean being able to practice their religion freely, to get a better job, or to live in peace.

67. Native Americans or American Indians

   Explanation: When the Europeans arrived in America, there were already hundreds of tribes of people living there. Today we call those people Native Americans.

68. Africans or people from Africa

   Explanation: Between 1619 and 1808, millions of Africans were brought to America and sold as slaves. In 1863, President Abraham Lincoln issued the Emancipation Proclamation which freed the slaves.

69. Any one of the following is correct: to have their own government, to stop paying high taxes (taxation without representation), because British army soldiers stayed in their houses without their permission (also known as boarding or quartering).

   Explanation: After over 100 years of English rule, the colonists wanted to govern themselves and make their own laws.

70. Thomas Jefferson

   Explanation: Jefferson wrote the Declaration of Independence in June of 1776, summarizing the reasons the colonists wanted and deserved to be free from British rule.

71. July 4, 1776

   Explanation: The Declaration of Independence was adopted by the Continental Congress after three days of making changes to Jefferson's original.

72. Answers will vary, but must contain three of the following: New Hampshire, Massachusetts, Rhode Island, Connecticut, New York, New Jersey, Pennsylvania, Delaware, Maryland, Virginia, North Carolina, South Carolina, Georgia.

   Explanation: The colonies were formed from 1607 (Virginia) to 1733 (Georgia), and joined together to rebel against British rule.

73. either the Founding Fathers wrote the Constitution, or the Constitution was written

   Explanation: The Constitutional Convention, or Philadelphia Convention, was a gathering of 55 delegates from several states. The delegates are known as the Founding Fathers.

74. 1787

   Explanation: It took four months for the Constitutional Convention to write the Constitution.

75. Any one of the following is correct: James Madison, Alexander Hamilton, John Jay, or Publius.

   Explanation: All of the essays making up the Federalist Papers were signed "Publius," but most people believe they were written by Madison, Hamilton, and Jay.

76. Any one of the following is correct: U.S. diplomat, oldest member of the Constitutional Convention, first postmaster general of the United States, writer of *Poor Richard's Almanack*, started the first free libraries.

   Explanation: One of the Founding Fathers, Ben Franklin had many talents and made important contributions to our country.

77. George Washington

   Explanation: Washington is known as the Father of Our Country because he was the first president.

78. The Louisiana Territory or Louisiana.

   Explanation: President Thomas Jefferson bought the Louisiana Territory, doubling the size of the country, and making westward expansion possible.

79. Any one of the following is correct: War of 1812, Mexican-American War, Civil War, Spanish-American War.

   Explanation: More Americans lost their lives fighting wars in the 1800s than in the five wars the United States fought in the 1900s.

KAPLAN

80. The Civil War or the War Between the States

   Explanation: The Civil War divided the country between Northern states and Southern states that broke away from the United States and formed the Confederacy.

81. Any of the following is correct: slavery, economic reasons, states' rights.

   Explanation: Southern states wanted to keep their slaves and Northern states wanted to free them. The economy in the South depended on slaves, who had to work without being paid. The Southern states also wanted to protect their right to make their own laws in case the federal government made slavery illegal.

82. Any of the following is correct: freed the slaves; freed slaves in the Confederacy, Confederate states, or most Southern states.

   Explanation: Signed by Abraham Lincoln in 1863, the Emancipation Proclamation freed the slaves, who were being held in Southern, or Confederate, states.

83. Either answer is correct: fought for women's or civil rights

   Explanation: Susan B. Anthony believed all Americans should have the same rights whether they were men or women. She worked to get women the right to vote, campaigning and leading protests.

84. Woodrow Wilson (or Wilson)

   Explanation: Woodrow Wilson served as president from 1913-1921.

85. Franklin Roosevelt (or Roosevelt)

   Explanation: Franklin Roosevelt served as president from 1933-1945, leading the country out of the Great Depression and through World War II.

86. Germany, Japan, and Italy

   Explanation: Japan's bombing of Pearl Harbor brought the United States into World War II, but Japan had formed an alliance with Germany and Italy known as the Axis Alliance. Therefore, America fought against not just Japan but its allies as well.

87. World War II

   Explanation: Eisenhower was commanding general of our military, leading them to victory in World War II. He served as president for two terms, from 1953-1961.

88. Communism

   Explanation: After World War II, the Soviet Union began taking over countries and making them Communist. The United States wanted to stop the spread of Communism. The conflict between the Soviet Union and the United States was called the Cold War because it was never fought directly.

89. the civil rights movement

   Explanation: In the 1950s and 1960s, African Americans began to protest the way they were being treated. They became organized under the leadership of Dr. Martin Luther King Jr., and worked to gain their civil rights.

90. the United States was attacked by terrorists

   Explanation: Terrorists took over four passenger planes, crashing two into the World Trade Towers in New York, and one into the Pentagon in Washington. The fourth plane crashed in a field in Pennsylvania.

91. Any one of the following is correct: Cherokee, Navajo, Sioux, Chippewa, Choctaw, Pueblo, Apache, Iroquois, Creek, Blackfeet, Seminole, Cheyenne, Arawak, Shawnee, Mohegan, Huron, Oneida, Lakota, Crow, Teton, Hopi, Inuit.

   Explanation: When the Europeans came to America, there were already millions of people living here. Native Americans, or American Indians, lived throughout what is now the United States in many different tribes.

92. Either is correct: the Missouri River or the Mississippi River

   Explanation: The Missouri River, at 2,540 miles is the longest river in the United States. The next longest is the Mississippi, at 2,340 miles.

93. the Pacific Ocean

   Explanation: California, Oregon, and Washington make up the West Coast of America, and are on the Pacific Ocean.

94. the Atlantic Ocean

    Explanation: Maine, New Hampshire, Rhode Island, Massachusetts, Connecticut, New York, New Jersey, Delaware, Maryland, Virginia, North Carolina, South Carolina, Georgia, and Florida make up the East Coast of America and are on the Atlantic Ocean.

95. Any one of the following is correct: Puerto Rico, U.S. Virgin Islands, American Samoa, Northern Mariana Islands, Guam.

    Explanation: Territories are lands that are under United States law but keep their own governments. People living in territories other than American Samoa are considered United States citizens.

96. Any one of the following is correct: Maine, New Hampshire, Vermont, New York, Pennsylvania, Ohio, Michigan, Minnesota, North Dakota, Montana, Idaho, Washington, Alaska

    Explanation: Thirteen states border Canada, the northern country on the continent of North America.

97. Any one of the following is correct: California, Arizona, New Mexico, Texas

    Explanation: There are four states that share a border with Mexico, the country to the south of the United States.

98. Either answer is correct: because the stripes represent the original 13 colonies; because there were 13 original colonies

    Explanation: The flag began with 13 stripes and 13 stars. As the number of stars grew each time a state was added, the number of stripes stayed the same.

99. the "Star-Spangled Banner"

    Explanation: The lyrics for the "Star-Spangled Banner" are from a poem written by Francis Scott Key during the War of 1812. It was set to music and adopted as the national anthem in 1931.

100. Any two of the following are correct: New Year's Day, Martin Luther King Jr. Day, Presidents' Day, Memorial Day, Independence Day, Labor Day, Columbus Day, Veterans Day, Thanksgiving, Christmas

    Explanation: The United States celebrates eleven national holidays. The last one to be added was Martin Luther King Jr. Day in 1986.

Glossary

Many of these terms are found on Form N-400, and on the English and Civics tests during your interview. Be sure you understand each one; use a dictionary to find the definitions of new words, and study those that are not familiar to you.

allegiance—Loyalty to a nation. When you say the Pledge of Allegiance, you promise to be loyal to the United States.

allies—Countries that fight a war on the same side. Our allies during World War I were England and France. In World War II, our allies were Russia, England, and France.

amendment—A change to the Constitution. Currently there are 27 amendments.

Anthony, Susan. B—a proponent of equal rights for women; fought for a woman's right to vote.

April 15—the date federal income tax forms must be sent by.

Atlantic Ocean—The body of water on the east coast of the United States.

Bill of Rights—The first 10 amendments to the Constitution, which protect individuals' freedoms and limit the power of the federal government.

Boston Tea Party—A protest by colonists against the taxes England was making them pay.

cabinet—The president's advisors.

Capitol building—The place where Congress meets in Washington, DC.

checks and balances—Provided by separating the power of the federal government into three branches; each branch can "check" on the others to make sure they are working the way they are supposed to, and that power is balanced among all three.

citizen—Someone who by birth or naturalization owes loyalty to a country and is protected by it.

Civil Rights Amendment—The Fourteenth Amendment, passed after the Civil War, which gave African Americans full rights as citizens.

Civil War—The conflict between Northern free states and Southern slave states fought from 1861—1865.

Colonists—people who came to America prior to 1776 to be able to freely practice their religion, enjoy better economic opportunities, and/or to escape persecution.

Communist—form of government of the former Soviet Union and the United States' main concern during the Cold War.

Cold War—The "war" between the Soviet Union and the United States that was never fought directly.

Congress—The legislative branch of the federal government that makes laws. Congress is made up of the House of Representatives and the Senate.

Constitution—The document that explains our laws, our government, and the powers of the government. It is also called the supreme law of the land.

continuous residence—The length of time a permanent resident lives in the United States without taking a long trip out of the country. Most people who apply for naturalization need five years of continuous residence.

Declaration of Independence—The document that explained to England that the colonies wanted to rule themselves. It was written mainly by Thomas Jefferson and adopted by the colonies on July 4, 1776.

Democratic Party—one of the two major political parties in the United States (the other is Republican).

Eisenhower, Dwight—former World War II general who served as President from 1953-1961.

Electoral College—A group of electors from each state that officially chooses the president about a month after the general election in November.

Emancipation Proclamation—An order issued by President Lincoln during the Civil War to free slaves in the 11 confederate states.

England—The country where the first colonists came from, and which ruled the colonists until it was defeated in the Revolutionary War.

executive branch—Headed by the president, the branch of the federal government that carries out laws, commands the armed forces, and directs foreign policy.

Father of our Country—The name given to the first president, George Washington.

fingerprint—An impression of the fingertip made in ink. Fingerprints are taken after you file Form N-400, the Application for Naturalization. They are used for identification because no two people's fingerprints are alike.

Form N-400—The Application for Naturalization.

Franklin, Benjamin—one of the founding fathers. Franklin signed the Declaration of Independence and the Constitution.

freedom of the press—A right guaranteed to American citizens by the Bill of Rights; it states that the federal government cannot control the press, or media.

freedom of religion—A right guaranteed to American citizens by the Bill of Rights stating that citizens can practice any (or no) religion without interference by the federal government.

freedom of speech—A right guaranteed to American citizens by the Bill of Rights ensuring that citizens can say or write their opinions without interference by the federal government.

free states—States that did not allow slavery. Most free states were in the North, and fought in the Union army during the Civil War.

governor—The elected head of a state.

Great Depression—The time during which the United States economy was very weak, beginning with the stock market crash of 1929 and ending with the New Deal programs of President Franklin Roosevelt.

House of Representatives—Part of Congress; made up of 435 elected representatives who serve two-year terms. The state's population determines the number of representatives the state has in the House.

immigrant—Someone who leaves one country to live in another.

Independence Day—The holiday celebrating America's independence from England, celebrated each year on July fourth.

interview—A meeting with someone from the USCIS after you file form N-400. In the interview, you go over your application and take the English and Civics tests.

Jamestown—The first English colony located in what is now Virginia.

Jefferson, Thomas—The third president and main writer of the Declaration of Independence.

Johnson, Andrew—Abraham Lincoln's vice president, who became president after Lincoln's assassination. He was in office during the period after the Civil War known as Reconstruction.

judicial branch—The part of the government that interprets the Constitution. It is made up of the court system, including the Supreme Court.

July fourth—The day Americans celebrate the country's independence from England.

Kennedy, John F.—The president during the civil rights movement in the early 1960s.

King Jr., Dr. Martin Luther—A leader in the civil rights movement.

Korean War—fought in the 1950s to try to stop the spread of Communism.

legislative branch—The part of the government that makes laws. It includes the Senate and House of Representatives.

Lincoln, Abraham—The president during the Civil War; he freed the slaves.

Louisiana Purchase—The land deal in which President Jefferson bought the Louisiana Territory from France, doubling the size of the United States.

Mexican-American War—1846 dispute about Mexican land that ended with the United States gaining what is now the American Southwest, from Texas to California.

Mississippi River—The body of water flowing north to south that divides the United States.

moral character—The kind of person you are. To be eligible for citizenship, you must be of good moral character. If you committed a certain type of crime, you may not be eligible to become a citizen.

Native Americans—People who were already living in America when the colonists landed.

naturalization—The way an immigrant becomes a citizen of the United States.

naturalization oath ceremony—After your application is accepted, you take the oath of allegiance and become a United States citizen.

New Deal—Government programs started by President Franklin Roosevelt to end the Great Depression in America.

Nineteenth Amendment—The 1920 change to the Constitution giving women the right to vote.

oath—A promise. When you say the oath of allegiance to the United States, you promise to renounce foreign allegiances, support the Constitution, and serve the United States.

passport—A government document that proves citizenship and allows you to travel to other countries.

Pearl Harbor—An American military base bombed by the Japanese in 1941. The next day, the United States entered World War II.

permanent resident—Someone who has permanent resident status according to immigration law. He or she has a permanent resident card. After five years, a permanent resident can apply for naturalization.

Persian Gulf War—fought by the United States and other countries in 1991 to force Iraq to leave Kuwait, which it had invaded.

Pilgrim—A Protestant who left England to have religious freedom.

Pledge of Allegiance—A promise said by Americans showing loyalty to the flag and "the republic for which it stands."

Police Protection—service provided by state governments as explained in the Constitution.

Poll Tax—once charged to keep poorer citizens from voting; a Constitutional Amendment makes charging such as tax a crime.

Presidents' Day—one of the 11 federal holidays celebrated in the United States.

Publius—name used to sign all of the Federalist Papers, which were printed to support the Constitution.

Republican Party—one of the two major political parties in the United States (the other is Democratic).

Reagan, Ronald—The president during the end of the Cold War.

Reconstruction—The time of rebuilding after the Civil War. Southern states made it very difficult for freed slaves by taking away their rights.

republic—The kind of government we have in the United States.

Revolutionary War—The war fought by the colonists against England to gain their independence.

right to bear arms—A guarantee of American citizens given in the Bill of Rights.

Roosevelt, Franklin—The president who served four terms beginning in 1933. His New Deal programs helped America recover from the Great Depression.

segregation—The practice of separating black and white Americans, and denying blacks the same opportunities as whites had.

Senate—The part of Congress made up of 100 senators (two from each state) who serve six-year terms.

Separation of Powers—the three branches of government divide power and prevent any one branch from having too much power.

September 11, 2001—date of the terrorist attacks in New York and Washington that killed almost 3000 people.

slave states—States where it was legal to own slaves until the Civil War. Slave states were in the South, and left the Union when Lincoln was elected, forming the Confederate States of America. They fought against the free states in the Civil War, lost the war, and once again became part of the Union.

Spanish-American War—conflict in which Spain fought to keep control of Cuba, Puerto Rico, Guam, and the Philippines. They lost to the United States, which claimed all of those territories.

Speaker of the House—leader of the House of Representatives who becomes President of both the President and Vice-President cannot serve their complete terms.

"Star-Spangled Banner"—The national anthem, written by Francis Scott Key in 1814.

Supreme Court—The highest court in the United States, made up of nine justices who are appointed by the president to lifetime terms.

supreme law of the land—The Constitution.

term limit—The restriction on the number of years a president can serve (two terms).

Thanksgiving—A holiday first celebrated by the Pilgrims and Native Americans after their first successful harvest.

13 colonies—The original group that came together to declare independence from England and form the United States of America.

Underground Railroad—A system that helped slaves in the South escape to freedom, in which people guided and hid the slaves until they reached a free state.

United Nations—A group of countries that came together after World War II to try to prevent more wars and to give aid to poorer countries.

United States Citizenship and Immigration Services (USCIS)—The government agency that helps immigrants become citizens.

veto—The president's power to refuse to sign a bill into law.

War of 1812—America's "second war of independence" against England.

Washington, George—The first president of the United States.

Washington, Martha—The wife of the first president, George Washington.

White House—The home of the president and his or her family. The White House is at 1600 Pennsylvania Avenue in Washington, DC.

Wilson, Woodrow—The president during World War I who came up with the idea for the League of Nations.

World War I—The conflict between allies including France, England, Russia, Italy, and the United States and their enemies, including Germany. The United States entered the war after Germany destroyed an American submarine.

World War II—The conflict between allies including France, England, and the United States and their enemies Germany, Italy, and Japan. The United States entered World War II after Japan bombed its naval base in Pearl Harbor.

NOTES